LIVING THE EUCHARISTIC MYSTERY

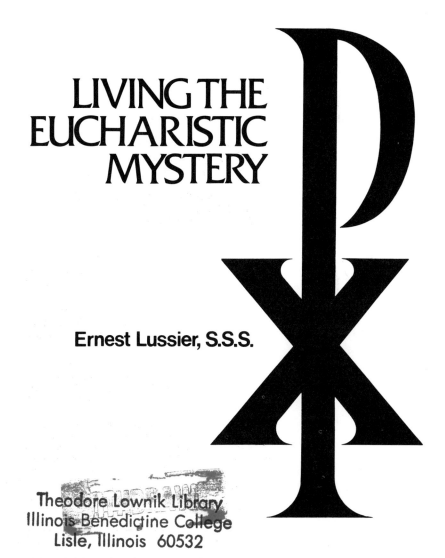

LIVING THE EUCHARISTIC MYSTERY

Ernest Lussier, S.S.S.

A L B A · H O U S E   NEW · YORK

SOCIETY OF ST. PAUL, 2187 VICTORY BLVD., STATEN ISLAND, NEW YORK 10314

Library of Congress Cataloging in Publication Data

Lussier, Ernest, 1911-
Living the Eucharistic mystery.

1. Lord's Supper—Catholic Church. I. Title.
BX2215.2.L88   234'.163   75-22027
ISBN   0-8189-0322-8

Imprimi Potest:
Normand Falardeau, S.S.S.
Provincial

Nihil Obstat:
Daniel V. Flynn, J.C.D.
Censor Librorum

Imprimatur:
+ James P. Mahoney, D.D.
Vicar General, Archdiocese of New York
July 11, 1975

The Nihil Obstat and Imprimatur
are a declaration that a book or pamphlet is considered
to be free from doctrinal or moral error. It is not implied that
those who have granted the Nihil Obstat and Imprimatur agree
with the contents, opinions or statements expressed.

Designed, printed and bound in the United States of
America by the Fathers and Brothers of the Society of St. Paul,
2187 Victory Boulevard, Staten Island, New York, 10314,
as part of their communications apostolate.

1 2 3 4 5 6 7 8 9 (Current Printing: first digit).

DEDICATION

To the Virgin Mary

Mother of adorers

in spirit and in truth

with tender devotion

and unswerving veneration

INTRODUCTION

In the Constitution on the Liturgy, the Fathers of the II Vatican Council, reflecting the clear teaching of Sacred Scripture and of the Council of Trent said: "At the Last Supper, . . . Our Saviour instituted the Eucharistic Sacrifice of His Body and Blood. He did this in order to perpetuate the sacrifice of the Cross throughout the centuries until He should come again, and so to entrust to His beloved spouse, the Church, a memorial of His death and resurrection, a sacrament of love, a sign of unity, a bond of charity, a paschal banquet in which Christ is consumed, the mind is filled with grace, and a pledge of future glory is given to us" (no. 47).

The Council Fathers also explained that "The most blessed Eucharist contains the entire spiritual wealth of the Church, that is, Christ Himself, our pasch and living bread, by the action of the Holy Spirit through His very flesh vital and vitalizing, giving life to men" (PO no. 5).

In the Encyclical Letter, "Mystery of Faith," Pope Paul VI exhorted priests to "tirelessly promote the cult of the Eucharist, the focus where all other forms of piety most ultimately emerge."

Responding to this exhortation, Father Ernest Lussier, S.S.S., in an earlier work, *Getting to Know the Eucharist*, treated primarily of the doctrine concerning the Holy Eucharist. In the present volume, *Living the Eucharistic Mystery*, he endeavors to provide a doctrinal stimulus to a greater appreciation of the Blessed Sacrament in our daily lives and to a more fervent Eucharistic piety. Father Lussier wants us to love the Eucharist more. We can never love the Eucharist—Our Lord—enough, because our finite love, even when most intense, cannot equal his infinite love for us.

This book is being published at the threshold of the Forty-first

International Eucharistic Congress which will be celebrated in Philadelphia. In announcing the Congress His Holiness Pope Paul VI stated: "To all the hungers of the human family the Eucharistic Congress will offer with confidence and loving faith, the only—the perfect solution, Jesus Himself who said: "I am the bread of life. He who comes to Me will never be hungry and he who believes in Me will never thirst" (Jn 6:35).

Father Lussier expresses the fervent hope that this volume will serve "as a preparation for the 41st International Eucharistic Congress" which, as all such Congresses, is intended to manifest our faith in the Holy Eucharist, to serve as a means of intensifying and spreading faith in the Eucharist, and to serve as a stimulus for attaining the goals suggested by its theme.

It is my fervent hope that this book, which reflects Father Lussier's deep confidence and loving faith in our Eucharistic Lord, not only fulfill the author's intentions of preparation for the Congress, but also generate anew and preserve devotions to the Blessed Sacrament. May it intensify devotions such as the Forty Hours, holy hours, private visits to our Eucharistic Lord and a more fervent and frequent participation in the Eucharistic Sacrifice.

My best recommendation of this volume cannot possibly match the merits of its contents. A prayerful reading of it will help the reader to achieve a more intimate life in Christ, and appreciate the reality that the Eucharist is the source and summit of Christian life, which essentially is a Eucharistic life.

JOHN CARDINAL KROL
Archbishop of Philadelphia

April 30, 1975

AUTHOR'S PREFACE

Getting to Know the Eucharist as described in my first book (Alba House 1974) is just a first step leading to *Living the Eucharistic Mystery* as here presented. Christ is our living bread, a bread that he gives us that we may live in him, as he lives in the Father. By eating this bread we already have eternal life, the sure hope of living forever (Jn 6:51-58).

Earthly bread is the staple of our human life. Prayer, the desire to receive God within ourselves, is clearly the essential element of Christian living, the bread of our spiritual life. Now, all prayer, liturgical or contemplative, is Eucharistic. It is directed to the Eucharist, receives its value from the Eucharist, has its summit, explanation, and perfect realization in the Eucharistic celebration and Holy Communion. "The most blessed Eucharist contains the Church's entire spiritual wealth, that is, Christ himself, our Passover and living bread. Through his very flesh, made vital and vitalizing by the Holy Spirit, he offers life to men." "No Christian community can be built up unless it has its basis and center in the celebration of the most Holy Eucharist" (P O nos. 5 and 6).

The material offered here is not meant to be read straight away, but rather in a meditative spaced-out fashion. It might easily serve as resource data for Eucharistic homilies, for Holy Hours and special occasions like first communions and first Masses. May it also serve as a preparation for the 41st International Eucharistic Congress to be held in Philadelphia, Aug. 1-8, 1976. The emblem for the Congress is a host surrounded by two hands, with the caption "Jesus, the Bread of Life. The Eucharist and the Hungers of the Human Family."

ERNEST LUSSIER, SSS.

CONTENTS

First bread in the Old Testament: bread as a gift of God, the fruit of man's labor, daily bread, shared bread, bread offered, and the bread of the Divine Word. Likewise wine, which is a cause of human joy, yet involves danger through excessive use. Wine was also offered in sacrifice.

The second part considers bread and wine in the life of Jesus who eats and drinks as men do. He is the living bread, the new wine. At the Last Supper Jesus uses bread and wine making them the sacrament of his redemptive sacrifice. Finally, an examination of bread and wine in the primitive Church.

Jn. 6:58 summarizes the teaching of the whole discourse on the bread of life. Starting from the miracle of the loaves, with the help of a few biblical concepst and images (the manna, the wisdom banquet) which he explains and spiritualizes, Jesus reveals himself as the true Messiah who brings eternal salvation precisely because he comes from heaven, lives by the Father (57) and gives his flesh for the life of the world (51). He is the bread of life in all that he does but in a special, privileged way in the sacrament of the Eucharist (51-58).

Commentary on 1 Cor 10:16-17, 12:12-27; Ep 1:23, 3:14-23, 4:4-5. The Pauline thought on the Body of Christ expresses the basic revelation of Paul's experience on the road to Damascus: the risen Christ lives in his own by faith, by baptism and especially by the Eucharist.

The Eucharist is deeply rooted in the mystery of the Blessed Trinity. It is the great thanksgiving to the Father, the gift and memorial of Christ, and the gift also of the Holy Spirit whose invocation renders Christ really present and gives him to us to transform our life. Gift of God, the Eucharist is celebrated in the Church whose life it is. The Eucharist summarizes the history of our salvation. Christ is the sacrament of our encounter with God; the Church is the sacrament of Christ; and we Christian should be the sacrament both of Christ and of his Church.

Christ's Eucharistic presence is not an empty word, a superstition, or an imaginary myth, but a sacred reality beyond human comprehension and accepted uniquely by faith. It si the personal presence of Christ as incarnated, as our redeemer, our victim and our prist, living, life-giving, even glorious. The Eucharistic gift is an act which summarizes all his life, recapitulates the whole history of salvation and brings it to its final fulfillment.

The Eucharistic mystery is woven into the mystery of the Incarnation and of the Redemption. It is the living synthesis of revelation. The Eucharist is a recapitulation of Christ's saving mission, its complete fulfillment. All Christ's relations with men in their world and their history are thus gathered together, and are signified and fulfilled by his presence in the Eucharist.

Eucharistic theology and devotion have taken important new orientations. The social and ecclesial aspects of the Eucharistic celebration are now better understood, as also its Paschal, memorial, covenant, in one word, its eschatological character, based on the sacramental nature of the Eucharistic presence.

Whether our new liturgical possibilities are considered risks or opportunities will depend to a great extent on our individual mentality, sensibilities, or even prejudices. The post-Vatican II renewal of the Mass emphasizes its essential character as an assembly of God's people in which everyone is invited to co-operate, to express himself and identify himself with the celebration. The liturgy is the best Church school, the best catechetical instrument the Church has at its disposal.

The Instruction *Eucharisticum Mysterium* on Eucharistic Worship (May 25, 1967) insists on re-centering all aspects of the Eucharist around the community celebration of the Eucharist as memorial of Christ's death and resurrection. To this must be added its insistence on the revaluation of hte Word of God in the liturgical celebration where word and sacrament should be understood together. This theology also develops a better understanding of the different modes of the presence of Christ to his Church. It would seem that the only possibility of survival for Eucharistic devotions lies in their integration with the Eucharistic liturgical celebration of the Mass. Recent Instructions from Rome.

The general Instruction which prefaces the new Sacramentary (1970) gives an excellent summary of the actual Eucharistic faith of the post-Vatican II Church. The new Roman Missal puts in better perspective within a wider framework of doctrine and practice the traditional faith of the Church in the sacrificial character of the Mass, in the real presence of Christ under the Eucharistic species (without prejudice to his other real presences in the liturgical celebration) and faith in the unique role of the ministerial priest. A special feature of the new order of the Mass is found in the periods of social silence.

Eucharistic spirituality could be described as the mind of Christ (1 Cor 11:24) and the logic of the Spirit (Jn 6:63) directing and inspiring our reactions to the Eucharistic mystery. The problem of the tension between the love of God and the love of neighbor, that we find in present-day spirituality, appears also in our Eucharistic practice as one between the supernaturalist and the secularist views. There is no reason, however, why both views, the transcendentalist and the naturalist, could not be coordinated. All symbols are more or less relative and need more or less interpretation.

The theology of the Eucharist has been reinterpreted in more secularized sense but this should be done in complete fidelity with the essential elements of the Eucharistic mystery. The Eucharist is essentially a reference to Christ in the Paschal act of his death and resurrection and the participation of all Christians in this mystery. An authentic Eucharsit must therefore include the desire for union with God, the effort to realize union with all men, and the hope which transcends death, all of this through Christ, with him, and in him.

The Eucharist should be the taproot in which Christian and priestly living finds its nourishment. A priest especially, but also to some extent every Christian, should live the Eucharistic celebation as a high point in his life, and should appreciate personal mental prayer as a joyful encounter with God, preparing and extending into his life the grace of the Mass.

By the Eucharist the Church is most fully and perfectly itself, the people of God, the community of worshipping believers, the body of Christ, the heavenly city, the new Jerusalem.

The Eucharist and religious faith and practice are practically inseparable. The Church must be a human community before being a Christian community. The Christian experience involves the whole of human life and experience. Our Eucharistic communion will be authentic only if we give the world a full and true interpretation of Christ's gospel. The Eucharistic celebration is the ecclesial and human foundation, source, and ultimate realization of our Christian faith.

The Eucharistic assembly is the major assembly of the Christian people in which they find their deepest meaning and greatest effectiveness. It is an assembly entirely based on faith, a community of conversion built on repentant love, a community of adoring love, of fraternal love, the assembly of God's glory. Christ is the rock foundation of the Christian Eucharistic assembly by his actual presence and action in which are present the past mystery of the Cross-Resurrection, the actual mystery of the assembly of salvation, and the future mystery of the eschatological assembly at the time of the Parousia.

In the three stages of God's revelation of himself to the world (the Old Testament, the Incarnation, the Church) it is possible to distinguish three specific modes of relation of the Holy Spirit to the Word of God: maturation, manifestation, expansion. In a special way in the Eucharistic mystery the gfit of the Holy Spirit is constantly renewed in the Church. Our Eucharistic celebration should be marked as a permanent Pentecost. The epiclesis (invocation) of the Spirit on the assembly and on the Eucharistic elements expresses the total and constant life-situation of the Church.

The forgiveness of sins is the power to receive God and rejoice in his presence in union with Christ. The Eucharist "the blood of the covenant poured for the forgiveness of sins" (Mt 26:28) is par excellence our God-given means to celebrate: the sacrament of promise, hope and joy. Eucharistic people find their joy in God which is what thanksgiving (Eucharist) is. Genuine celebration is real thanksgiving. The word Eucharist is a term associated with a celebration, a feast, a festival. The Eucharist is thanksgiving, a memorial and celebration of God's wonderful saving deeds in our behalf. Christ makes God real to us but also makes us real, truly human beings, loving God and loving God's people.

In assuming our common humanity, the Word of God united himself with all of humankind, so that there are no human limits to the identification of the Christ of the Eucharist with the one world of human beings. Because he si preeminently the man who is the model of all men, nothing human is alien to him. The Eucharist is an effective symbol of the renewal of all things by Christ and in Christ. Real liturgy and a sense of awareness of the Christian responsibility for society are mutually interdependent, like the love of God and the love of neighbor (Mt 22:37-40). The fellowship and the community which the Eucharist creates is unversal.

There are many ways in which Christ is really present to his Church, accomplishing the work of our salvation (when the Church prays, performs works of mercy, by grace in those who believe, in the proclamation of God's word, in the exercise of authority, and in the administration of the sacraments) but the heart of it all is his substantial, personal, premanent presence under the Eucharistic species. Far from obscuring the essential Eucharistic mystery of the Mass and of Holy Communion,

Eucharistic devotions actually spring from the Liturgy and pre-pare for a richer liturgical participation.

Man's essential duty to God can be stated in one word, worship which is reverence and service of God. Now prayer is one of the essential elements of worship, another being sacrifice which is external worship. Prayer is of its very nature worship. Prayer gives worship its spirit and its truth. There are in the Old Testament a succession of great prayer—hymns which are, as it were, the backbone of biblical revelation.

Acclamation, proclamation, blessing, and the hymn are the biblical forms of the prayer of praise and adoration.

Examines the biblical texts relative to the divinity of Christ. Jesus is one of the divine Persons enumerated in the Trinitarian formulas (2 Cor 13:13).

The Apocalypse is the gospel, the proclamation and accla-mation of the Risen Christ, a gospel of adoration and worship. Christ is assimilated to and identified with God, worthy of the same honor and adoration.

Direct non-exclusive prayer to Jesus is rightful because of the unity of nature and action in the divinity which theologians call the interchange of attributes: Christ is both God and man. The use of Kyrios for Jesus in the early Church bestowed on him the ineffable divine name of Yahweh. The New Testa-ment doxologies, having a liturgical, cultic background, are consequently especially important in the study of the development of the expression of direct prayer or cult to Jesus. The Trinitarian doxology, as we know it, is the perfect expression of worship, the three divine persons being treated on a basis of equality: "Glory to the Father, and to the Son, and to the Holy Spirit" (cf. Cor 13:13).

John, but especially Paul, suggest the different facets of Christ's influence on the life of Christian believers by using pregnant prepositional phrases to express the intimate union between Christ and the Christian. Four of these phrases deserve special attention: through Christ, into Christ, with Christ, and in Christ. One will recognize here the substance of the great Eucharistic doxology.

The first Christians lived in common and prayed in common with the breaking of the Eucharistic bread as the central ceremony of their worship (Ac 2:42). The reason for the efficacy of the prayer of the community is the presence of Jesus (Mt 18:19-20) whose prayer the Father always hears (Jn 11:42). He is the amen of our faith (Rv 3:14).

In praise of prayer, especially before the Blessed Sacrament. Our prayer life like Christ's should be a transfiguration, a momentary exhilaration preparing us for the Christian mission. It is unreal and presumptious to believe that one can sustain true Christian service without the kind of supporting prayer life that Christ himself exemplified and taught. Prayer without action is not enough, and action without prayer will soon wither and die. Action that is prayer results only from prayer.

St. Eymard considered the Eucharistic sacramental union as the end and purpose of all our Lord's mysteries, the end also of the Christian life and virtues. His special charism, the guiding idea of all his priestly activity was the Eucharist: Eucharistic worship and apostolate.

The Eucharist is the sacrament of salvation today, the sacrament of Christ reaching all men in our time and all times. It is a meal which here below is never finished. Our Eucharistic celebration is the actualization here and now of the mystery of our redemption in its totality: from the Incarnation to Pentecost, passing by the inseparable mystery of Christ's death and resurrection as the summit of his salvific action, to Christ's final coming at the end of time. It commits us to share in Christ's saving gesture in order that his life may prevail over all the forces of alienation and of death. We must humanize people before they can be evangelized and sacramentalized.

List of Abbreviations

DV—*Dei Verbum*
Dogmatic Constitution on Divine Revelation

EM—*Eucharisticum Mysterium*
Instruction on Eucharistic Worship

LG—*Lumen Gentium*
Dogmatic Constitution on the Church

OT—*Optatam Totius*
Decree on Priestly Ministry

PO—*Presbyterorum Ordinis*
Decree on the Ministry and Life of Priests

SC—*Sacrosanctum Concilium*
Constitution on the Sacred Liturgy

LIVING THE EUCHARISTIC MYSTERY

One

THE EUCHARISTIC BREAD AND WINE – I

When Jesus at the Last Supper took bread and wine making them his own body and blood and giving them as food to his disciples, these humble elements already had a long biblical background. They are often mentioned in the Old Testament, and Jesus himself in his public life often referred to them and used them. The study of the biblical themes of bread and wine will then be of great help to understand the Eucharistic mystery. After seeing the meaning of bread and wine in the Old Testament, we shall consider the use Jesus made of bread and wine and the place held by bread and wine in the life of the first Christians.

The first mention of bread in the Bible is found in the dramatic context of the condemnation of man after the fall. "In the sweat of your brow you shall eat bread till you return to the ground out of which you were taken" (Gn 3:19). Man's labor is his way of collaborating with God's bountiful gifts. This is repeated in the beautiful psalm of creation: "You make grass grow for the cattle, and plants for man to cultivate, that he may bring forth bread from the earth" (104:14). Plenty and famine are interpreted as divine recompense or punishment: "I have never seen the righteous forsaken or his children begging for bread" (Ps 37:25). And when the wise man speaks of man's work, "He who tills the soil will have plenty of bread" (Pr 12:11), he is not thinking only of the natural efficacy of man's labor. The worker is the friend of God who recompenses man's diligence by the fertility of the land.

The prophets often underline that famine is the punishment for sin, like hard work in Genesis (3:18-19). When Ezechiel announces that God "will break the staff of bread in Jerusalem" (4:16) this is clearly a punishment deserved for sin. "Does evil befall a city unless the Lord has done it" (Am 4:6)?

Bread, being a gift from God, must be prayed for and expected with confidence. Many biblical episodes illustrate the need of this interior attitude. In the wilderness the Hebrews were given the manna (Ex 16:15) which biblical tradition soon qualified as "bread from heaven" (Ps 105:40), "the bread of angels" (Ps 78:24-25) because it manifested quite clearly God's action. By the ministry of Elisha one hundred men are fed with "twenty barley loaves and and fresh ears of grain" (2 K 4:42-44). The formula "Thus says Yahweh, they shall eat and have some left" (43) indicates that the bread is God's gift and that superabundance is characteristic of the divine bounty.

Quite naturally the perfect happiness which God prepares for us at the end of time is described by the biblical authors as a superabundance of bread: "He will give rain for the seed you sow in the ground, and the bread which the ground provides will be rich and nourishing" (Is 30:23). The Israelite saw bread as the fruit of his labor but especially as a gift from God, and received it with gratitude.

Many texts show that bread is man's *daily* food. The expression to eat bread is equivalent to take a meal, to nourish oneself. "Cursed be the man who eats bread before evening, before I have had my revenge on my enemies" says Saul as he imposes an absolute fast as a means of winning God's gift, victory (I S 14:24). And just as to eat bread means to nourish oneself, so also to live, the different situations and attitudes of life are presented in refer- to bread. "You have fed them with the bread of tears" sings the Psalmist (80:6) as he recalls the misfortunes of Israel, especially the exile. Isaiah also speaks of "the bread of adversity" (30:20). Qohelet (9:7) advises his reader to seek the bright side of life: "Go eat your bread with joy, and drink your wine with a glad heart." The wicked eat "the bread of wickedness" (Pr 4:17) and the lazy "the bread of idleness" (31:27). The delicacies of a well garnished table are "bread of deceit" (23:3) because of the excesses to which they may lead. Thus a fundamental need of our human nature becomes part and parcel of biblical terminology and theology.

The ancient bread was normally broken, to be eaten and *shared* with others. Bread became the means of human communication and communion. Hence the Psalmist's tragic reflection: "Even my bosom friend in whom I trusted, who ate of my bread, has lifted his heel against me" (41:10).

The duty of hospitality was sacred in Israel, as it still is in Arab culture. In the theophany to Abraham at Mamre, we find a typical and touching example of biblical hospitality. The patriarch insists, "Let me fetch a little bread and you shall refresh yourselves before going further" (Gn 18:5). To share one's bread with the hungry was an instant recommendation and an expression of Hebrew piety. "A blessing awaits the man who is kindly, who shares his bread with the poor" (Pr 22:9). In his portrait of the just man, the one who has reached moral perfection, Ezechiel places a condition that "he gives his own bread to the hungry" (18:7). The author of Job underlines the perfection of his hero when he has him state: "Have I taken my bread alone, not giving a share to the orphan" (31:17)? Shared bread is "the fast which pleases the Lord" (Is 58:6).

In gratitude to its Creator, Israel offered God bread which thus became an *object of worship*. To bring to God at the harvest feast the first fruits of the crop was an ancient custom (Ex 23:16, 19). Later when the cultic duties of the community were codified, Leviticus speaks of the first fruits of bread to be offered at the time of the feast of Weeks, which was held seven weeks or fifty days after the Passover (hence its Greek name, Pentecost) and marked the end of the wheat harvest. "You shall bring from your dwellings two loaves of bread; they shall be of fine flour and shall be baked with leaven, as first fruits to the Lord" (Lv 23:17). This bread was ultimately given to the priest (23:20), an indication of its sacred character.

Already in ancient times, in the Israelite sanctuary, a certain number of bread loaves were placed on a table and considered as consecrated to Yahweh. The bread was called presence (literally, bread of the face, I Sam 21:6) bread or showbread because it was placed before the presence of Yahweh in the ark. Other names for it were holy bread (I S 21:4, 6), continual bread (Nb 4:7) and loaves of proposition or setting up (Ch 9:32). This custom of setting bread before the deity was very common in the ancient Orient and represented feeding the God. Only the priests in Israel could consume these loaves when they were replaced by fresh, warm bread (I S 21:7).

In Solomon's time the loaves were placed on a golden table (I K 7:48). The priestly legislation underlines the importance of the rite by giving the details for the fabrication of the table (Ex 25:23-28) as well as for the confection of the loaves (Lv 24:5-9).

They were to be placed in permanence before Yahweh (Ex 25:30), twelve of them, covered with incense and renewed each Sabbath (Lv 24:8). Their purpose was not as in pagan cults to feed the divinity; the God of Israel refuses human nourishment (Jg 13:16). They expressed the people's (the number twelve symbolizes the twelve tribes) intention to give thanks to God at all times for the food he gave them. They were thus an acknowledgment of God's continuing bounty to his people and also the symbol of the covenant, the communion between God and Israel (Lv 24:8).

Another rite was also very important in Israelite worship, that of unleavened bread. Leaven because of its fermenting power was often considered as a symbol of corruption (1 Cor 5:7) and consequently sacrifices were usually accompanied by unleavened bread. "You must not offer leavened bread with the blood of the victim sacrificed to me" (Ex 23:18). "No cereal offering which you bring to the Lord shall be made with leaven" (Lv 2:11).

To sanctify the great spring festival called the feast of Unleavened Bread (Massot) the Israelites ate unleavened bread for a week (Ex 23:15). This ancient agricultural feast originally celebrated the offering of the first fruits of the barley harvest but was soon joined to another ancient pastoral feast for the offering of the firstborn of the flocks, a feast which became the Passover. Both of these feasts were then associated with a historical occurrence, that decisive event in the history of Israel's election, the deliverance out of Egypt, and the rites took on an entirely new religious significance: they recalled how God had saved his people (Ex 12:26-27, 13:8).

This symbolism of the unleavened bread is explained in relation to the Exodus but differently in different texts. In Ex 12:39 "it was not leavened because thrust out of Egypt, they could not tarry, neither had they provided for themselves any provisions." In 12:8 it is a bread of misery eaten with the bitter herbs to recall the hard Egyptian servitude. A suggestion of renewal is found in 12:15 where it is a new bread prepared for the feast, probably like the original agricultural idea of a new era ushered in by the new harvest.

The Jewish Passover, which now includes the feast of Unleavened Bread, because a rehearsal for the Christian Passover. Christ the Lamb of God, was sacrificed on the Cross and given as food to his disciples at the Last Supper in the atmosphere and background of the Jewish holy week of Passover. Thus he brings salvation to the world; and the mystical re-enactment of this redemptive act becomes the central feature of the Christian liturgy, organized around the Mass which is at once sacrifice and sacrificial meal.

Christ crucified, our Passover, our Paschal Lamb is the one sacrifice for all. The Christian is united with the sacrificed and risen Christ in an unending Passover; he must therefore remove the old yeast, that is evil and wickedness, and use unleavened bread, that is sincerity and truth instead. "Christ, our Passover, has been sacrificed; let us therefore celebrate the festival, not with the old leaven, the leaven of malice and evil, but with the unleavened bread of sincerity and truth" (I Cor 5:7-8). Single-mindedness should distinguish the Christian, a transparent purity of purpose and character.

The prophets, considering *God's word* as the spiritual food of the faithful, compare it to bread. In a terrifying but wonderful oracle the prophet Amos cries out: "Behold the days are coming, says the Lord God, when I will send a famine on the land, not a famine of bread, nor a thirst for water, but of hearing the word of God" (8:11).

Deuteronomy compares the word of God to bread in reference to the gift of manna. "He fed you with manna which neither you nor your fathers had known, to make you understand that man does not live on bread alone but that man lives on everything that comes from the mouth of God" (8:3). If bread fails God can ordain something else such as the manna. God creates all things by his word and so gives us life by means of his commandments which issue from his mouth. This passage from the material food to the spiritual, that is, obedience to God's commandments, is implicit in Deuteronomy and clearly suggested in our Lord's quote (Mt 4:4) at the time of his temptation. Later, speaking about the true bread from heaven Jesus stated: "The words I have spoken to you are spirit and they are life" (Jn 6:63). The Eucharist, the true manna from heaven (Jn 6:50) is the source of life for men. The revelation of the Eucharist is a message (words) of eternal life (6:68).

Man lives by God's commandments, a bread found in the prophetic revelation (Is 55:2-3) and in a special way in Wisdom, the teaching of the wise men of Israel. Personified Wisdom, the doctrine of life, God's word communicated to men, is presented as man's bread. "Come and eat my bread, drink the wine I have prepared. Leave your folly and you will live, walk in the ways of insight" (Pr 9:5-6). In John 2 and 6, Christ not only gives the wine of wisdom and the bread of teaching but also his sacrificial flesh and blood.

Briefly then the biblical theme of bread in the Old Testament shows that bread, the work of man's hands, still is a gift from God and places us in his dependency. Bread is a daily necessity of life and should be shared among men who are all dependent on God. Bread, the staff of man's life, is also offered to God in a gesture of adoration and thanksgiving. Finally, bread raises our hearts to another food, God's own word, divine Wisdom. This is the historical and spiritual background in which Jesus took the Eucharistic bread in his sacred hands at the Last Supper.

Already in some quotes we have seen that bread and wine are often mentioned together. Wine, however, for bible people was not the usual beverage but served for special occasions and references made to it by the inspired authors deserve special attention.

As for bread it is in a dramatic scene that we find the first biblical reference to *wine*. Noah plants a vine and is surprised by the effects of the wine he drinks. "Noah was the first tiller of the soil. He planted a vineyard; and he drank of the wine and became drunk and lay uncovered in his tent" (Gn 9:20-21). God's gift could evidently be put to shameful use. Noah's unhappy experience will be renewed in the course of history by people who unlike the patriarch have no excuse for their drunkenness. And so we find the invectives of the prophets against this vice and the satirical portraits of the sages along with their good advice.

The prophets inveigh against the leaders who in their cups forget their duty to God and to their people. "Woe to those who from early morning chase after strong drink and stay up late at night inflamed with wine . . . but have no regard for the works of the Lord or see the work of his hands" (Is 5:11-12). They are too sotted with wine to give a thought to God. Drunkenness is disapproved especially because of the religious indifference it occasions.

The intoxicating wine cup appears as the symbol of the divine punishments against the nations or even Jerusalem. "Yahweh the God of Israel said to me: 'Take from my hand the cup of the wine of wrath and make all the nations to whom I send you drink it. They shall drink and stagger and lose their wits at the sword I am sending them' " (Jr 25:15-16). This idea of the cup of suffering or bitter experience is frequent in the Old Testament and evidently focuses on the after effects of carousing and not on the immediate joys of drinking.

The sages often warn their disciples against the effects of drunkenness: indigence, stupidity, debauchery, and violence. "He will not grow rich who loves wine and good living" (Pr 21:17). "Your eyes will see strange things, distorted words will come from your heart" (twisted fancies and irresponsible speech) (Pr 23:33). "Wine and women corrupt sensible men" (Si 19:2). "Drunkenness increases the anger of a fool to his injury, reducing his strength while leading to blows" (Si 31:30). Wine must then be used with discretion. "Wine is life for man if drunk in moderation" (Si 31:27).

The need for sobriety has led certain personages to a more or less total abstinence from wine mostly for religious motives. The priests must not take wine or strong drink when exercising their functions (Lv 10:9, Ezk 44:21). The clan of the Rechabites in fidelity to ancient custom practiced total abstinence (Jr 35:6). The Nazirites who consecrated themselves to God by special vow abstained from wine: so Samson (Jg 13:4-5) and possibly Samuel (I S 1:11). At a later date the nazirite vow could be temporary but always included this abstinence. "He shall abstain from wine and strong drink and neither drink the juice of grapes, nor eat grapes, fresh or dried" (Nb 6:2-3). The culture of the vine and the use of its products were a characteristic of the Canaanites with whom the children of Israel had been commanded to hold no intercourse.

Yet the dangers of wine and the necessity for moderation in its use (Pr 20:1) did not completely obliterate from the biblical mind the positive aspect of wine as the symbol and the servant of innocent joy and happiness (Ps 4:7, Jn 2:1-11).

There are texts which express the *joy of wine* in man's life. In the ancient piece known as Jotham's fable, the vine is invited to reign over the other trees but declines saying: "Must I forego my wine which cheers the hearts of gods and men to stand swaying above the trees" (Jg 9:13)? This is an anti-royalist satire of the monarchy. Olive, fig, and vine, trees of value refuse kingship as serving no useful purpose; the thornbush, fruitless and noxious accepts it. The great psalm of creation also states that wine "makes men happy" (Ps 104:15).

The sages who guard men against the abuse of wine, nonetheless underline the joy wine affords when taken in moderation at a joyful banquet. "What is life worth without wine? It was created to make men happy" (Si 31:27). "An emerald seal in a golden setting, such are strains of music with a vintage wine" (Si 32:6). Wine, music, and song have their place along with words of wisdom.

An atmosphere of joy accompanied the vintage which was characterized by rejoicing, songs and dances (Jg 9:27) and the joyful shouts of the grape-gatherers (Is 16:10). Because it generates carefree joy, wine symbolizes all that is agreeable in life like friendship and love. "How sweet is your love; how much better than wine" (Sg 4:10). "New friend, new wine. When it grows old, you drink it with pleasure"(Si 9:10).Old friends are like old wine. Wine must age; time proves the worth of friendship.

In general wine symbolizes all the joy available here below. It is the image used by Zechariah to evoke future joy: "Ephraim will be like a hero, their hearts will be cheered as though by wine" (10:7). And so the religious symbolism of wine leads up to the eschatological future. When the prophets announce divine punishments, they threaten a lack of wine. "Though they plant vineyards, they shall not drink from them" (Zp 1:13). "You shall tread grapes but not drink wine" (Mi 6:15). "You shall plant vineyards and dress them, but you shall neither drink of the wine nor gather the grapes; for the worm shall eat them" (Dt 28-39).

On the other hand, the oracles of consolation which paint the portrait of a time of perfect, messianic peace predict a superabundance of wine. "They will come and sing aloud on the heights of Zion and they shall throng toward the good things of the Lord, grain, wine, and oil, sheep and oxen; . . . they will sorrow no more" (Jr 31:12). "Come buy wine and milk without money and without price" (Is 55:1). "Behold I am sending you grain, wine and oil, and you will be satisfied" (Jl 2:19). "How good and how fair it will be! Grain shall make the young men flourish and new (sweet) wine the maidens" (Zc 9:17). The fruitfulness of the Palestine of the coming age is a divine blessing providing abundantly the fruits of the earth for an increasing population.

Along with the bread and the victims for sacrifice, wine also takes a place in Old Testament worship. It is *offered as a libation*. At the sanctuary in Shiloh, Hannah, the mother of Samuel, brings a skin of wine with a three-year-old bull and an ephah of flour (I S 1:24), probably the customary offering for the redemption of a first-born son. The sacerdotal legislation gives some specifications for the use of wine in sacrifices. "You must make a libation of wine, one quarter of a hin to each lamb in addition to the holocaust or sacrifice" (Nb 15:5). The quantity of the wine increases according to the size of the animal sacrificed: a third of a hin for a ram (15:7) and a half for a bull (10). A hin is about one quart. Nothing is said here concerning the manner of this rite. In ancient Greece and Rome the custom was to pour the wine over the sacrificed animals, and some have assumed that this was the Israelite custom also. According to Si 50:15 the drink offering was poured out at the foot of the altar.

In the apocalyptic poem in Is 63:3 the divine vengeance against Edom is compared to a vintage scene; the juice flowing from the wine press figures the blood of the pagans struck by God. "I have trodden the wine press alone. . . . In my anger I trod them down and trampled them in my wrath; their life-blood is sprinkled upon my garments and all my clothes are stained." The Fathers often applied these lines to Jesus in his bloody death on the cross, but the poet speaks here of the wicked man's blood on the garments of the divine conqueror. This wine presser has nothing in common with the Servant of Yahweh. A similar scene is found in Rv 14:19-20.

The symbolism of wine in the Old Testament is then ambiguous. Wine can figure the sin of man but it can also be seen in the plan of God's creation as an expression of joy and a symbol of the great eschatological happiness which finds its realization in the messianic coming of our Lord.

Two

THE EUCHARISTIC BREAD AND WINE – II

When we open the New Testament, first of all the Gospels, we find that bread and wine are not mentioned very often. What we do have, however, is all the more precious to understand the revelation of the Eucharist.

One point is clear. *Jesus eats bread and drinks wine* like anybody else. Unlike John the Baptist his asceticism does not include restrictive alimentary practices. "John came neither eating nor drinking and they say, 'He has a demon;' the Son of Man came eating and drinking and they say, 'Behold a glutton and a drunkard, a friend of tax collectors and sinners' " (Mt 11:18). Jesus was poor and preached renunciation, he befriended sinners and the outcasts but made no radical departure from the usual manner of life of the Jews.

He is often shown eating and drinking with his friends (Jn 2:1-11), with publicans and sinners (Mk 2:15-17), with the Pharisees (Lk 7:36). He accepts man's ordinary food but religiously, knowing that it is God's gift. He wants his disciples to ask God for it every day: "Give us this day our daily bread" (Mt 6:11). We must ask God for the sustenance we need in this life but for no more, not for wealth or luxury. The beautiful development on trust in divine providence places us in this perspective: "Do not be anxious about your life, what you shall eat or what you shall drink" (Mt 6:25). Passing from the material bread to our spiritual bread, the Fathers easily applied the petition for bread to the bread of the Holy Eucharist.

By multiplying the loaves in the wilderness and by changing the water into wine at Cana, and always in superabundance, Jesus

shows that he is the instrument of a God who has compassion on
man's material difficulties in life. "I feel sorry for these people;
they have been with me for three days and have nothing to eat.
I am unwilling to send them away hungry; they might collapse
on the way" (Mt 15:32). The formulas, "they all ate and were
satisfied" (Mt 14:20); "And they filled them up to the brim"
(Jn 2:7), underline the liberality of Christ's gift on the material
plane and already prepare for the revelation of the bountiful
Eucharistic bread.

Jesus tells his disciples not to take along provisions on their
missionary tours since God by the intermediary of those who are
evangelized will furnish what is necessary. "Take nothing for your
journey, no staff, nor bag, nor bread, nor money" (Lk 9:3). Jesus
recommends ascetic poverty and reliance on God and not on one's
own resources, having in view also the traditional hospitality of
the people. All the more so since material food, though necessary,
must not make us forget the spiritual food of God's word. This is
intimated by our Lord in his temptation in the wilderness as he
rejected the devil's suggestion to change stones into loaves of
bread. "Man does not live on bread alone but on every word that
comes from the mouth of God" (Mt 4:4). The symbolic meaning
of bread is clearly suggested.

In the episode of the Canaanite woman who is begging for the
cure of her daughter, Jesus answers: "It is not right to take the
children's bread and throw it to the dogs" (Mt 15:26). This is a
little parable. Jesus must devote himself to the salvation of the
Jews, the children of God and of the promises before turning to
the pagans. The bread represents the salvific action of the Messiah.
The benefits of Jesus' ministry, his words and actions are a nourishing bread.

Special attention must be given to the multiplication of the
loaves (Mt 14:13-21). The fact that there are five parallel passages
shows that the event had made a strong impression on the first
Christian generation. The miracle is also prominent in the gospel
presentation since in all four gospels it marks the climax of Jesus'
Galilean ministry (Mk 6:31-54, Lk 9:10-17, Jn 6:1-15). Whether
Mt 15:32-38 and Mk 8:1-10 really deal with a second multiplica-

tion of loaves or are simply a traditional doublet is a critical problem of minor importance.

In the synoptic gospels the miracle is evidently put in relation to the Last Supper. In all the texts the actions of Jesus as he multiplies the loaves are described in the terms found later in the narrative of the institution of the Eucharist. "He took the five loaves and the two fish, raised his eyes to heaven and said the blessing. And breaking the loaves he handed them to his disciples" (Mt 14:19). For the Evangelists the miraculous bread, though not the Eucharist, clearly prefigures and leads up to it. It is a messianic sign and symbol which will find its fulfillment in the true messianic banquet, the Eucharist. It is because Jesus is the *bread of life*, offered and shared, that he is able to feed the people with abounding generosity. "I came that they may have life and have it abundantly" (Jn 10:10) is an intermediary explanatory text.

Mark and Luke gave the miracle in a context of teaching. "As he stepped ashore he saw a large crowd; and he took pity on them because they were like sheep without a shepherd, and he began to teach them many things" (Mk 6:34). "He spoke to them of the kingdom of God" (Lk 9:11). Historically the understanding of the symbolism of the miracle of the loaves must have been bread as the divine word, the living teaching of Jesus, as is strongly emphasized in John's gospel (Ch 6), a first step up to the higher Eucharistic meaning.

In John's gospel the miracle is situated in a Paschal atmosphere: "The passover, the feast of the Jews was at hand" (6:4). And by placing the discourse on the bread of life after the multiplication of the loaves the Johannine tradition clearly means to enlighten one by the other. This is done, as it were, in two overlapping waves in the wonderful discourse. The affirmation of Jesus, "I am the bread of life," is first developed in the sense of the bread of faith, the living word of God. This theme of faith dominates the first section (Jn 6:35-47). "He who comes to me shall not hunger; and he who believes in me shall never thirst" (35). "He who believes has eternal life" (47). The loaves are first the image of the word of God communicated by Jesus to nourish our faith.

In a second wave (Jn 6:48-58) the same statement, "I am the

bread of life," is developed in the sense of Eucharistic bread. Jesus is the living bread because in a mysterious manner he gives himself as food to his disciples. "Anyone who eats of this bread will live forever: and the bread which I will give is my flesh for the life of the world" (6:51). The word flesh suggests a connection between the Eucharist and the Incarnation: the Word made flesh (Jn 1:14) is the food of man. Jesus is the true bread because he is God's Word of revelation, the Father's message which he passes on to man (3:11), but also because he is a victim whose body and blood are offered in sacrifice for the life of the world (6:15). To be nourished with the bread of life is to participate in Christ's sacrifice. The full understanding of our Lord's intention and teaching was reached in the light of the Last Supper by the faith of the post-resurrection Church under the action of the Holy Pentecostal Spirit.

Two important texts, one from the synoptic catechesis (Mt 9:14-17), the other from the Johannine tradition (Jn 2:1-11), present Jesus as *the new wine*. The disciples of John the Baptist, like the Pharisees, used to observe fasts not prescribed by the law in the hope that their devotion would hasten the coming of the kingdom. One day they came to Jesus asking: "Why is it that we and the Pharisees fast, but your disciples do not? Jesus replied: '. . . new wine is not put into old wine skins; if so the skins burst and the wine is spilled and the skins are destroyed; but new wine is put into fresh skins and so both are preserved' " (Mt 9:14-17).

The old skins stand for Judaism in so far as it contains elements which in the scheme of salvation are to pass away. The new wine represents the new spirit of the kingdom of God, Jesus himself, his message, his work of salvation. The super-added devotional practices of John's disciples and of the Pharisees intended to give new life to the old order, but in fact were only leading to its downfall. Jesus refuses either to add or to patch; his purpose is to produce something quite new. Even the spirit of the law is to be raised to a new plane (5:17f).

Just as wine gives men joy so also Jesus by his presence brings the messianic joy, he dispenses the new wine of the messianic banquet. "Can the wedding guests mourn as long as the bride-

groom is with them" (Mt 9:14)? Christian fasting at its highest
is an expression of sorrow for the Passion of the Lord and for our
present separation from him. Jesus, the new wine, comes to change
the history of the world and to bring joy. But the new wine he
provides was not appreciated by those who had drunk the old wine
of the law. "Nobody who has been drinking old wine wants new.
The old is good he says" (Lk 5:39). Pious conservatism prevented
their accepting the new revelation. Actually the old and the new
seldom meet peacefully: think of the problems between the Jewish
Christians and the Gentile Christians in the early Church. The final
saying of Luke seems to restrain one from completely rejecting
the old; the new to be palatable must contain the genuine spirit of
the ancient law.

In the light of this parable we can better understand the deep
meaning of the miracle at the wedding at Cana (Jn 2:1-11). No
doubt the unexpected abundance of the wine symbolizes the coming of messianic times. In Nb 13:23f, the spies bring back a bunch
of grapes from the promised land. Here Jesus manifests his glory
(11) with the implication that the wine is the symbol of the new
age. Jesus is at the same time the new spouse of Israel and the
abundant new wine replacing the water of Judaism. John notes
that the jars served for the Jewish rites of purification (6) suggesting that he sees in them an image of Judaism. The reflexion of
the steward of the feast should be interpreted in this perspective.
"You have kept the good wine until now" (10). Israel has long
awaited the Messiah but now he is here; by his person, his action,
his message, he is the good wine.

The miracle appears also as a preparation for the institution of
the Eucharist. The mention of the mother of Jesus (2:1), like at
the foot of the cross (19:25) with its apparent reference to Gn
3:15, 20, presents Mary as the second Eve, the mother of the living. And the objection of Jesus, "My hour has not yet come"
(2:4), refers to our Lord's passion and resurrection, and includes
the Eucharist (13:1). This hour is determined by the Father and
cannot be anticipated, but the miracle worked through Mary's
intervention is a prophetic symbol of it.

Thus the wine at Cana is a distant image of the blood of Christ, just as the multiplied loaves prepare us for the revelation of Christ's Eucharistic body. The good wine is destined for the believers who unite themselves to Christ in person.

The allegory of the vine in St. John's gospel (15:1-8) has also a Eucharistic overtone, especially in view of the Last Supper setting of this discourse. In the synoptics Jesus uses the vine as the symbol of the kingdom of God (Mt 20:1-8, 21:28-31, 33-41) and the fruit of the vine becomes the Eucharistic sacrament of the new covenant (Mt 26:29). The union between the branch and the vine can be seen as a figure of the Eucharistic communion of believers with Christ and among themselves. The Eucharistic union should bear fruit and deepen the union between Jesus and his disciples already existing through love.

In this background of the biblical themes of bread and wine, we more easily understand the beauty and richness of the rite which Jesus instituted before his passion. Notwithstanding its sobriety, due to a stereotype necessitated by liturgical practice, the narrative of the *Last Supper* is rich in biblical reminiscences.

Jesus takes bread (Mt 26:26) and a cup containing the fruit of the vine (26:27-29) to symbolize effectively his redemptive passion. The bread becomes "my body given for you" on the cross (Lk 22:19); and the wine is "my blood, the blood of the covenant, which is poured out for the forgiveness of sins" (Mt 26:28), "the cup of the new covenant in my blood, which will be shed for you" (Lk 22:20). But beyond this essential reference to the Paschal mystery we should also hear all the overtones of the biblical tradition relative to bread and wine.

The Eucharistic bread and wine are par excellence the gift of God; and Christ assumes for his sacrifice this bread and wine, the fruit of man's labor. It is the bread shared by the multitude who believes in Jesus, a bread which unites them all together in one communion. It is bread offered not only in homage and thanksgiving but as a true sacrifice. And because it gives us Christ, the living Word of God, the Eucharistic bread is also the bread of the Word, wisdom food come down from heaven. The Eucharistic wine is the wine of joy, which transforms man's heart and renews his energies.

To mark the continuity between the Last Supper and the religious meals of the old covenant, especially the Paschal Supper, the Passover, and at the same time to indicate its novelty, Jesus took bread and pronounced a blessing over it (Mt 26:26). This must have been a prayer to his heavenly Father similar to the blessings found in the Old Testament and in contemporary Judaism. Jesus gave thanks to God as every pious Jew did over bread and wine. The grace before partaking of bread in the Jewish daily prayer book was the following: "Blessed are you, O Lord our God, King of the universe, who bring forth bread from the earth;" and before partaking of the wine, "Blessed are you Creator of the fruit of the vine." Such a blessing evidently would obtain a more sublime meaning on the lips of our Lord, and include an appeal to the divine omnipotence. Notice how the Jewish blessings have been closely imitated in the offertory prayers of our new order of the Mass. The name Eucharist, given to the sacrament from antiquity, recalls Jesus' blessing and is quite appropriate since the eucharistic celebration is a memorial in praise of all God's wonderful works for our salvation.

Benediction is a spontaneous act of admiration before God's plan and naturally comprises recognition, praise, and thanksgiving for the gifts received. Many instances are found in the Bible, for example on the lips of Abraham's servant (Gn 26:26f) or of Jethro (Ex 18:19) or in Psalm 103, a hymn celebrating God's loving kindness.

Jesus must have had such prayers on his mind in his Eucharistic blessing. The gospel has preserved two blessings actually pronounced by our Lord, one called the great jubilation (Mt 11:25), the other his prayer before the tomb of Lazarus (Jn 11:41) where he thanks God for his mission as savior. Our Lord's discourse after the Last Supper (Jn 14:17) must be an elaboration of his prayer at the supper which announces the sacrifice of the Cross, the fulfillment of God's plan for our salvation.

Finally, a word must be said about the theme of bread and wine in the *primitive Church*. To the Thessalonians who, in the mistaken belief that the end of the world was at hand, had given in to laziness and idleness, giving up their normal employment, upsetting others and preventing them from working, St. Paul forcefully recommends what has been called the golden rule for Christian work. "We call on people of this kind to go on quietly working and earning the bread they eat" (2 Th 3:12). "We gave you a rule when we were with you: if anyone will not work, let him not eat" (10). This admonition is supported by an appeal to Paul's own example (7) who labored for his daily bread although he had the right to be maintained by the Church.

Encouraging the Corinthians to be generous in the collection in favor of the poor, Paul reminds them that God does not let his faithful lack bread. "He who supplies seed to the sower and bread for food will supply and multiply your resources and increase the harvest of your righteousness" (2 Cor 9:10). God will recompense even temporally the resources of the almsgiver.

For wine Paul echoes the advice for sobriety found in the Old Testament sapiential literature. Christians are not forbidden the use of wine. Timothy is told to "no longer drink only water but use a little wine for the sake of your stomach and your frequent ailments" (1 Tm 5:23). But excesses must be avoided. "Do not get drunk with wine for that is debauchery; but be filled with the Spirit" (Ep 5:18). There was abundant use of wine in the mystery cults and at times abuses even in Christian gatherings (1 Cor 11:21). Joyful fellowship should result not by escape into a world of artificial gaiety by drunkenness, over-drinking alcohol or as we might add today by taking drugs of various kinds, but rather from being filled with the Holy Spirit. The stimulus for effective living does not come from wine but from allowing the Holy Spirit full possession of our heart. Being filled with the Spirit is connected with joy, courage, spirituality, and character. The Christian alternative to the fun of getting drunk is not solemn dullness, but spiritual exhilaration.

Sobriety is one of the qualities required of the priest (1 Tm 3:2), of the deacon (8) and of older women (Tt 2:3). There are also cases when abstinence from wine must go further than ordinary prudence: if, for example, there was the risk of shocking less enlightened Christians. "In such cases the best course is to abstain from meat and wine and anything else that would make our brother trip or fall or weaken in any way" (Rm 14:21). The strong must restrict his own liberty if he finds his example is injuring a weaker brother, an age-old problem.

In the Apocalypse John uses the biblical image of wine (14:8-10) for the divine anger to which Babylon (Rome) has exposed all nations by making them worship her idols. Wine is also the symbol of the idolatry of Babylon. "All the nations have been intoxicated by the wine of her prostitution" (18:3).

An expression was current in the primitive Church, the *breaking of the bread* (Ac 2:42, 46, 20:7, 11, 27:35; Lk 24:30-35). In itself the phrase suggests a Jewish meal at which the one who presides pronounces a blessing before dividing the bread. For Christians, however, it implied the Eucharistic ceremony. This was celebrated not in the Temple but in private houses (Ac 2:46); the rite was accompanied by an ordinary meal (I Cor 11:20-24), the love feast (Jude 12).

St. Paul seems to allude to this expression in 1 Cor 10:16-17. "The cup of blessing which we bless, is it not a communion in the blood of Christ? The bread which we break, is it not a communion in the body of Christ? Because there is one bread, we who are many are one body for we all partake of the one bread." The cup of blessing is the cup of wine for which we thank God like Christ did at the Last Supper. By uniting us to Christ, the Eucharist unites us among ourselves to form Christ's mystical body.

Paul's narrative of the institution of the Eucharist (1 Cor 11:23-25) is a recall of apostolic tradition (23) and is closely parallel to the Lucan tradition (Lk 22:19-20). His approach is practical; he exhorts the Corinthians to a more dignified and charitable celebration of the Lord's Supper. More than the others he insists on the sacrificial character of the Eucharist; on the necessity of personal commitment as well as interior purity for the reception of the sacrament; and on its relation to the Parousia, its promise of the future triumph of the cause of Christ. "As often as you eat this bread and drink this cup you proclaim the Lord's death until he comes. Let a man examine himself before eating this bread and drinking this cup. For anyone who eats and drinks without discerning the body eats and drinks judgment upon himself" (1 Cor 11:26-28).

To conclude and summarize. Given to men by God for their nourishment and pleasure, bread and wine are naturally means of fraternal communion and of communion with God when they are offered in sacrifice. Jesus gave them a new value and meaning by taking them during his public life as symbols of his saving mission, and by making them at the Last Supper the sacrament of his redemptive sacrifice. As we eat our daily bread we should remember that we have another bread of which we are instantly invited to partake, our Savior himself, the lamb still bearing the marks of his sacrifice (Rv 5:6), our high priest "living forever to intercede for all who come to God through him" (Heb 7:25).

Three

BREAD OF ETERNAL LIFE

There can hardly be any doubt that Jn 6:51-58 refers to the Eucharist and presents Jesus nourishing our soul with his flesh and blood. Whether this passage is a later insertion into the narrative discourse contained in the rest of the chapter, does not alter the fact that we have here a true, authentic theology of the Eucharist surely elaborated according to the mind and intention of our Lord. Actually this section fits in beautifully with the rest of the chapter. Jesus reveals himself as bread of life in all his messianic activity but he is the bread of life in a very special manner in the Eucharist, which is the symbol and efficacious sign of our Savior. Nowhere else is Christ what he is so fully and so tangibly than in the Eucharist which is par excellence the sacrament of Christ, the bread of life, even if his redemptive activity extends beyond the framework of the sacrament and is not restricted to the sacramental rite. The Eucharist is a center which gives meaning and life, radiates or draws to itself all the works of redemption and spiritual living, not one which eliminates all the other sacraments, mysteries, or good works.

One of the major themes of John (ch. 6) is that of the *Son of Man* (27, 53), the enigmatic title which our Lord preferred and which no one else ever uses in reference to him. The phrase which originally meant simply man, a human being (Ezk 2:1) was nonetheless a title suggesting glory because of its use in Daniel's famous prophecy (ch. 7); it both veiled and hinted at the sort of Messiah Jesus was. Before Caiphas (Mt 26:64) our Lord, finally, made the whole situation clear: "You will see the Son of Man seated at the right hand of the Power and coming on the clouds of heaven."

He acknowledges that he is the Messiah but not as the human Messiah of traditional expectation but as the Lord of Ps 110 and the mysterious personage of heavenly origin whom Daniel had seen in a vision.

In the fourth gospel the expression Son of Man takes on added signification since it connotes Christ's divine origin. The formula is linked to an important Johannine antithesis: ascend-descend (Jn 3:13). Jesus descended from heaven to bring eternal life, participation in God's life, through being lifted up on the Cross, the symbol of his lifting upon the Ascension. His Ascension to his Father, Christ's glorification supposes his descent from heaven, his divine origin. His Ascension will both show that Jesus really came from heaven, and also establish him the Son of Man on his glorious throne. The only one who can speak authoritatively of heavenly things is the only person who has both come down from heaven and ascended into heaven, the Son of Man.

In John 6 the question of the divine origin of Christ is the object of the discussion between Jesus and the Jews. "It was not Moses who gave you the bread from heaven; my Father gives you the true bread from heaven. For the bread of God is that which comes down from heaven and gives life to the world" (Jn 6:32-33). "The Jews murmured at him because he said, 'I am the bread which came down from heaven'" (41). This question of Christ's divine origin is evidently basic to the credibility of his teaching, as the climax of the chapter will show. He has the words of eternal life because he is the Holy One of God (68), God's chosen envoy.

But why does Jesus have recourse to the metaphor of bread when he affirms his heavenly origin? The bread in question is the Jewish *manna*. The Messianic hope of the chosen people was linked with the expectation of a new appearance of the manna.

The Old Testament often recalls that God nourished his people in a miraculous way in the wilderness, and the Jews constantly thanked him for it in the Psalms and in the book of Wisdom. "The Lord said to Moses, 'I will rain bread from heaven and each day the people are to go out and gather the day's portion'" (Ex 16:4). The manna is described as a thin flake like hoar frost (Ex 16:14) in size, or as the small greyish-white seeds of coriander (31). Its appearance was like that of bedellium (Nb 11:7-8), a transparent resinous gum; and its taste like a honey cake (Ex 16:31) or cakes made with oil (Nb 11:8) and so symbolized the sweetness of God (Ws 16:21).

The reference is, no doubt, to the Arabic manna, a sweet and sticky substance excreted by insects sucking the sap from tamarisk bushes. From the leaves of the thicket the substance drops to the ground where it becomes somewhat firm in the cool of the night desert air, but melts away with the heat of the sun (Ws 16:27). The Bedouins still consider manna as a delicacy. This is the natural phenomenon which God apparently used for his own providential purpose.

"The manna was like coriander seed and its appearance like that of bedellium. The people went about and gathered it and ground it in mills or crushed it in pots and made cakes of it; and the taste of it was like the taste of cake baked with oil. When the dew fell upon the camp in the night, the manna fell with it" (Nb 11:7-9. "He rained manna to feed them, he gave them the wheat of heaven, he gave them the bread of angels, he sent them food in abundance" (Ps 78-24-25). The manna was the bread which had rained from heaven (Ex 16:4) and was consequently referred to as the bread of heaven (Ps 105:40), the bread of angels and the substance of God (Ws 16:20-21), meaning the bread brought by the angels and a subsistence supplied by God through their ministry.

"You gave them the food of angels from heaven, untiringly sending them bread ready to eat providing every pleasure and suited to every taste. For the sustenance you gave manifested your sweetness towards your children; and the bread ministering to the taste of whoever ate it was changed to suit everyone's liking . . . the agent of your all-nourishing bounty . . . It was melted when simply warmed by a fleeting ray of sun, to make it known that one must rise before the sun to give you thanks, and pray to you when the light begins to dawn; for the hope of an ungrateful man will melt like wintry frost and flow away like waste water" (Ws 16:20-29). This theological presentation of the manna is somewhat poetic and hyperbolic. For example, in Nb 11:4-6 the Israelites complain about the lack of variety involved in being constantly fed on manna. Our sapiential writer here probably starts from the fact that the manna was the food of the Israelites during their entire sojourn in the wilderness (Ex 16:35). He then indulges in poetry as he glosses on what a heavenly food should be like, apparently thinking more of the eschatological banquet which is described in Rv 2:17 as the hidden manna. The manna, hidden together with the ark of the covenant by Jeremiah (2 M 2:4-8), will be brought out as the food of those who are saved in the heavenly kingdom.

All through the eventful history of the Israelite people, the prophets and the sacred writers have idealized more and more the journey through the wilderness of Sinai. Hosea (2:16-22) presents it as the time of Yahweh's first espousal of his people, their honeymoon. And at the beginning of the Christian era, the Jews believed that in the last days, the days of the Messiah, the gift of the manna would be repeated. In John (ch. 6) Jesus fulfills this expectation in his offer of the bread of life. For the Rabbis the manna, which ceased "on the morrow of the Passover" (Jos 5:12), the first in the promised land, is kept in reserve in heaven until the coming of the Messiah (Rv 2:17) as the eschatological food par excellence. Hence the importance of the multiplication of the loaves in the context, and of the evangelist's remark, "Now the Passover, the feast of the Jews was at hand" (Jn 6:4).

Moreover, the Jews easily passed from manna considered as a material gift to the notion of the spiritual food of God's word. "He fed you with manna which neither you nor your father had known, to make you understand that man does not live on bread alone but that man lives on everything that comes from the mouth of God" (Dt 8:3). If bread fails God can ordain something else such as the manna. God creates all things by his word and so gives us life by means of his commandments which issue from his mouth and must be obeyed. "It is not the production of crops that feeds man but your word which preserves all who trust in you" (Ws 16:26).

In the synoptics there is no explicit relation placed between the multiplication of the loaves and the Messianic expectation of the new manna. John, on the contrary, insists that Jesus himself is the true manna. "What sign will you give to show that we should believe in you? What work do you do? Our fathers had manna to eat in the desert" (Jn 6:30f). The multiplication of the loaves surely cannot be compared with the manna of the Exodus. Something more wonderful than that is expected of one who claims to be the Messiah (Jn 6:14, 27)."Jesus answered: 'I tell you most solemnly, it is my Father who gives you the bread from heaven, the true bread . . . I am the bread of life; he who comes to me will never be hungry, he who believes in me will never thirst' " (Jn 6:32-35). The manna was a bread from heaven, it came down from heaven like rain or snow. God gives a superior bread, which really comes from heaven, the true bread from heaven. The opposite of the Johannine *true* is not *false* but *imperfect*, shadowy or unsubstantial. Christ is giving the bread of which earthly bread is but a sample, a symbol. He is giving the substance to which the Old Testament figures point, the eternal, divine realities to which material food can hardly be compared. This real bread from heaven is first of all Jesus' teaching. Jesus identifies himself as incarnate revelation. The phrase "which (or who) comes down from heaven" occurs seven times (6:33, 38, 41, 42, 50, 51, 58) in the discourse like a solemn refrain and serves to join together the presentation of Jesus as the bread of life in his teaching (35-49) and in his very person in the Eucharist (51-58). It is a popular reference to the Incarnation which was later incorporated into the Nicene Creed.

The idea of *life* is at the base of Johannine theology, but the concept of life and eternal life does not appear as something completely new in the fourth gospel. John uses these concepts in practically the same meaning as the Jews and first Christians, without much change.

In the Old Testament life is considered as the highest good, the synthesis of all other good things, like peace, prosperity, happiness; death on the contrary is the greatest calamity. God is essentially the living one, as the Old Testament name Yahweh suggests (Ex 3:13-15), namely the one who is, the unique, living and true God who has unlimited existence as opposed to the nothingness of the false gods (Is 42-8, Ps 115). Jesus especially in John (4:26, 6:20, 8:24, 28, 58, 13:19, 18:5, 8 and twice in the discourse on the bread of life, 6:35, 51) appropriates this name more or less explicitly, thus claiming to be the one incomparable savior, the goal of Israel's faith and hope. The phrase "I am" expresses the eternal being of Christ, his continuing and eternal existence, setting him on a level with God.

God creates and gives life and the bible promises a long and happy life here on earth to those who obey God's law (Dt 5:16). In the second century B.C. a new idea of life appears, a life distinct from earthly life which will not be destroyed by death but will last forever. This is how, for example, Daniel describes the eschatological victory of God's people. "At that time your people shall be delivered, every one whose name shall be found in the book of life. And the multitude of those who sleep in the dust of the earth shall awake, some to everlasting life and some to everlasting disgrace. And those who are wise shall shine like the brightness of the firmament; and those who turn many to righteousness like the stars forever and ever" (Dn 12:2-3). The reference is not only to the great name which the devout leave behind them, as in Ws 3:7 and Is 1:31, but to an eschatological transformation of the whole person into a glorified state.

In the book of Wisdom this eternal life is promised to the just, while the wicked are confounded because of the basic vanity and perversity of all their doings on earth. "Then the righteous man will stand boldly to face those who have oppressed him, those who made light of his sufferings. The hope of the ungodly man is like chaff carried by the wind, it is dispersed like smoke before the wind . . . But the righteous live forever and their reward is with the Lord" (Ws 5:1, 14-15). The man who practices virtue (1:15) is assured of immortality, "his hope is full of immortality" (3:4). The term immortality for the author is not simply fame with posterity, as in prior Old Testament thought, but unending existence, communion (Ps 16:11) with God, blessed immortality.

The pious Jews at the time of our Lord did not expect from God only a long and happy life here below in the promised land, but also recompense for their good deeds in the eternal life of

Messianic salvation. Eternal life is assimilated to the Messianic kingdom of which it appears as a constitutive element, its final phase, the kingdom of the Father. In Mark to enter into life (9:43) is synonymous to entering into the kingdom of God (47). So also in Matthew to inherit the kingdom prepared since the foundation of the world (25:34) is to enter into eternal life (46). To the kingdom of the Son, the Messianic kingdom on earth (Mt 13:4), there succeeds the kingdom of the Father (43) to whom the Son commits the elect whom he has saved (Mt 25:34, I Cor 15:24).

This is the perspective in which Christ is called "the prince of life whom God raised from the dead" (Ac 3:15), the one who leads his subjects to full life by imparting his own life to them, "our leader and Savior" (Ac 5:31). Jesus is the new Joshua leading his people into the promised land.

None of the New Testament writings explain better than the fourth gospel how Christ confers on us eternal life and how it is the Messianic gift par excellence. Jesus is himself the life, as he declares solemnly to Lazarus' sister. "I am the resurrection and the life. He who believes in me even though he dies will live and whoever lives and believes in me will never die" (Jn 11:25). The believer who dies will come to life not necessarily like Lazarus but certainly on the last day. And he who believes and thereby is truly alive (20:31) will never die; physical death is not the end of his life which is eternal. The man of faith has conquered death once and for all. Jesus is not only the agent of final resurrection, but gives eternal life even now. He is in his own person the victory over death, he is eternal life; and in him what was a future hope has become a present reality.

"I am the way, the truth, and the life" (Jn 14:6). Jesus is the way: in him we have access to the Father, he makes the Father known to the world (Jn 1:18). He is the truth, which alone pleases the Father (4:23f). He is the life: to know the Father present in the Son is eternal life (17:3). Through Christ, the true and living way, one comes into the possession of the Father which means the possession of truth and life.

This biblical notion of life plays an important role in John's discourse on the bread of life (ch. 6). In fact life is the only effect of Christ's saving action which is mentioned explicitly. "Do not labor for the food which perishes but for the food which endures the eternal life" (6:27). "This is the will of my Father that everyone who sees the Son and believes in him should have eternal life and I will raise him on the last day" (6:40). John balances exactly the two aspects of the Christian life, in present possession (come, see, believe) and future hope (life everlasting, resurrection). "This is the bread which came down from heaven, not such as the fathers ate and died; he who eats this bread will live forever" (6:58). St. Ignatius of Antioch describes the Eucharist as "the remedy which provides immortality." Notice also how Jn 6:58 summarizes the teaching of the whole discourse on the bread of life. Starting from the miracle of the loaves, with the help of a few biblical concepts and images (the manna, the wisdom banquet) which he explains and elevates, spiritualizes, Jesus reveals himself as the true Messiah who brings eternal salvation precisely because he comes from heaven and lives by the Father (57). And he is the bread of life in all that he does but in a special, privileged way in the sacrament of the Eucharist (51-58).

The Eucharist is par excellence the sacrament of union between Christ and the faithful. "He who eats my flesh and drinks my blood lives in me and I in him" (6:56). To have eternal life (54) is to be in close communion with Jesus, to enjoy a mutual indwelling. By the Eucharist complete and reciprocal indwelling between Christ and the believer is attained. Christ is at once the center and the circumference of the life of the Christian; the source from which it springs and the ocean into which it flows, its starting point and its goal. According to St. Augustine the twofold aspect of our life of union with God is illustrated by the two great images of the body and the temple: *"Manemus in illo cum sumus membra ejus; manet autem ipse in nobis cum sumus templum ejus."*

This is one of John's characteristic phrases to express the most intimate mutual fellowship and union. The phrase occurs again in chapter 15 where the image of the vine suggests the Eucharistic mystery. Christ is so closely united to his disciples that their union can be compared to that of the Son with his Father. "Abide in my love . . . Just as I have kept my Father's commandments and abide in his love" (15:10). The same is said here: "As the living Father sent me and I live because of the Father, so he who eats me will live because of me" (6:57). Our Lord is describing the chain of the sources of life. The life which the Father communicates to the Son passes to the faithful through the Eucharist. Communion with Jesus is really a participation in the intimate communion which exists between the Father and the Son. Jesus gives man a share in God's own life. The Father is the absolutely living one, the font of all life (5:26) in whom there is no element of death. Our union with Christ in holy communion is a true image of his union with the Father in the Holy Spirit. Notice that to eat Christ's flesh and drink his blood is to feed on Christ himself. And just as the Eucharist itself echoes the theme of the Covenant (Mk 14:24) so also the mutual indwelling of God and Jesus and the Christian reflects the same covenant theme, "You will be my people and I shall be your God" (Jr 24:7).

It should be clear that this union with Christ is not realized automatically but by faith. We must adhere freely and with all our heart to our Savior; we must believe. This notion of faith is just as central in John as in Paul (Rm 1:16). John's gospel is written "that you may believe that Jesus is the Christ, the Son of God, and that believing you may have life in his name" (Jn 20:31). Faith is man's essential activity (6:29), the one needed above all else and from which the rest will follow.

Faith, the total gift of man to God and a grace of the Holy Spirit, is presented by our Lord with different images. "If anyone thirst let him come to me and drink. As Scripture has said, out of his heart shall flow rivers of living water" (Jn 7:37-38). Jesus is the true water of life. In the Old Testament fresh spring water symbolizes the water which God gives, especially that of the Messianic age (Is 12:3). Christ's invitation (Jn 7:37) resembles that of divine Wisdom. "Those who eat me will hunger for more and those who drink me will thirst for more" (Si 24:21). In John we read, "He who comes to me shall not hunger and he who believes in me shall never thirst" (6:35). The two statements insist on different aspects of faith which satisfies but is always more and more desirable.

Jesus under a visible sign gives the believer his flesh to eat and his blood to drink (6:52). As an efficacious symbol of the life which the Son of Man brings us, Eucharistic communion is as indispensable to the Christian as faith itself. "Unless you eat the flesh of the Son of Man and drink his blood you have no life in you" (6:54). Our faith is expressed and nourished in the sacramental union; the Eucharistic grace is at the same time the cause and the effect of our adherence to Christ by faith.

Jesus is the bread of life (Jn 6:35, 48), the living bread (51), the source of divine life, grace. The expression the bread of life, the bread which gives life (33) recalls the tree of life of the earthly Paradise (Gn 2:9), a symbol of the immortality lost by original sin. The promises of eternal life (Jn 6:51, 58) are the counterpart of the condemnation pronounced over guilty man (Gn 3:22).

In the Eucharist, the Messianic promises are realized for our benefit. The Eucharist is not only a recall of the past, the memorial of Christ's death; it is not only a pledge of the eschatological salvation which will be ours at the time of our Lord's glorious return; it is also, and even above all, the active presence of our Savior himself actually reliving the past and anticipating the future. "He who eats my flesh and drinks my blood has eternal life and I will raise him up on the last day" (6:54).

The Johannine theology of the Eucharist appears perfectly coherent and of unequaled depth, yet it does not coincide purely and simply with the rest of the New Testament; just as the synoptic image of Christ is only a rough sketch of the Johannine or Pauline presentation of the Son of God. In chapter 6 John insists that it is in the Eucharist that we receive the plenitude of the Messianic salvation. In the Eucharist, the sacrament of Christ living among us, Christ exercises all his saving activity. There are, however, other titles besides "the bread come down from heaven," the bread of eternal life, by which Christ is presented to our faith and worship. He is the Suffering Servant (Is 53) who has given his life in ransom for the multitudes (Mt 20:28), the Lord who will return on the last day (I Cor 11:26), the Son of God seated at the Father's right (Ac 2:33-35), the Incarnate Word (Jn 1:14).

Actually far from creating opposition to these other Christological titles, the image of the heavenly manna receives its true and full significance by being understood in the light of these other titles; it refers back to them and takes its full meaning in their light. "The bread which I will give is my flesh for the life of the world" (Jn 6:51).

Four

THE BODY OF CHRIST

The typical Pauline figure of the Body of Christ expressing the identity of Christians with Christ appears first in I Corinthians, a letter in which Paul copes with the divisive Corinthian factions. Christ is not divided, Paul tells them, using the symbol of the unity of the body to formulate his teaching. The analogy of society as a single body with many parts was classical in contemporary Hellenism to suggest the moral union of citizens conspiring to achieve the common good of peace and well-being. Paul, however, does much more than to transfer the idea of body politic to Christian society. His concept of the Body of Christ brings back the memory of his conversion (Ac 9:5) and is deeply colored by his faith in Jesus whose body raised from the dead and given life by the Spirit (Rm 1:4) became the first-fruits of a new creation (I Cor 15:23).

The words spoken by our Lord at Paul's conversion, "I am Jesus whom you are persecuting," imply that Christians are somehow identified with the risen Christ. For St. Paul we are *bodily* united with Christ's risen body by baptism (Rm 6:4) and especially by the Eucharist (I Cor 10:16-17) which makes us members of Christ's body, united in such a way that together we form the Body of Christ, what is now called the Mystical Body. The qualifier mystical, however, is not found in Pauline literature and has a history of its own.

In I Cor 12:12-27 the figure of the Body of Christ as used by Paul hardly transcends the idea of moral union that should be found among Christian believers. The spiritual gifts enjoyed by the Corinthians should be used for the good of the community, not for its disruption. As all the members conspire for the good of the body, so it should be with us Christians who form Christ's Body (12). The way a human body gives unity to all its component parts is the way Christ as the unifying principle of his Church gives unity to all Christians who are his body. There is a close association between Christ's Body and the Holy Spirit (13). The Spirit is the internal principle of unity in the Church. The Spirit gives us to drink in baptism and in the Eucharist. In St. John (4:10) living, that is, spring-fresh water signifies the Spirit and to drink implies a very close communion.

The following points emerge from Paul's development in I Cor 12:12-31. Every Christian is a necessary member of the community (14-16). The body is not one member but many; every member of the body has a necessary function to fulfill. The variety that exists is highly desirable, in fact, indispensable.

Every Christian needs the help of every other Christian (17-22). The parts of the body are mutually dependent. Unless a body can move the area of vision is restricted, and without eyes the feet cannot be guided (21). The weakest, more delicate organs such as the eyes, or invisible organs such as the heart are really indispensable (22).

Particular respect and care should be shown to those members of the community who appear to be less important than the rest (23-25). We cover with special care some of our members, for example, the sex organs and the organs of excretion and in so doing we bestow more honor on them than on other members which we do not cover (23). Here Paul intends to humiliate the Corinthians. If they receive more gifts of a charismatic nature than do others, they have no cause for pride; it is because they are weaker than others. This seems to indicate that in point of fact the special effusions of the Spirit were rather common in the Corinthian Church, and that some glorified in them.

Every Christian is sympathetically involved in the prosperity or misfortune of his fellow-Christians (25-26). There is therefore no reason for the more distinguished members of the congregation to despise the humblest members or to ignore them, nor for the apparently less important ones to feel that they have no proper place in the life of the community. Here we may recall the beautiful words of St. Augustine: "The ear sees in the eye: the eye hears in the ear. The eye can say, the ear hears for me." Differences in the respective conditions of the various members of the community can and should make more manifest the unity that should exist among its members.

Since the gifts of the Spirit have been distributed by God, and since no one gift is possessed by every member of the Church, nor does any one member possess them all, there is no cause for coveting gifts one has not received. On the other hand, it is allowable to aim at acquiring the higher gifts (27-31). And love is the highest of all (I Cor 13).

Rm 12:4-5, like I Cor 12:12-25, does not suggest more than a moral union, the conspiring of individual members for the common good as in the body politic. I Cor 6:15, however, and especially I Cor 10:16-17 go much further than moral union. In I Cor 6:15 Paul warns against the defilement of man's body by sexual license. Paul is not referring to members of a society, but to members of Christ as a physical individual; the union he has in mind is not so much corporate as corporal. Christ's body is for Paul a metaphysical reality, which thanks to faith, baptism, and especially the Eucharist, already extends its sway to the physical sphere where the future body of the resurrection is being prepared.

This is clearly suggested in 1 Cor 10:16-17 where Paul insists on the union of all Christians which is brought about by their share in the Eucharistic bread and cup: "though there are many of us, we form one body because we all share in the one bread." The unity of all Christians is derived from their consumption of the one Eucharistic bread. Through eating the bread and drinking the cup, Christians are united to Christ in an intimate fellowship because the Eucharist is his body and blood (11:27-31). From this Eucharistic fellowship with Christ follows the real union of all the faithful with one another in one body. Baptism incorporates the Christian into the body of the risen Lord; the Eucharist in which each communicant receives the body of Christ strengthens and cements this union. The Eucharist is consequently the *"sacramentum unitatis ecclesiae"* (St. Augustine) and when we receive the Eucharistic bread, Christ assimilates and transforms us, making us his Body. There is but one Eucharist, one Body of Christ which is not only a symbol but a sacrament, an effective sign of the unity which exists among the members of the Church who partake of the one bread.

This realistic teaching is taken up later on by Paul in the letters of the captivity, where the basic idea remains the same, that is, humans are reconciled to God by becoming living parts of Christ's body (Ep 5:30) which was physically dead but is now spiritually alive (Ep 2:14-18, Col 1:22). The stress, however, is now on the unity of the body that brings all Christians together in one Spirit (Ep 2:4), and on the identification of the body with the Church (Ep 2:22-23). Having thus personified the body (Ep 4:12) Paul asserts that Christ is the head (Ep 2:22 etc.).

The Church is explicitly identified with the Body of Christ in formulations that are almost convertible. "Christ is the head of the body, the Church" (Col 1:18, 24). "God made him the supreme head of the Church which is his body" (Ep 1:23). Ep 4:4-6 deserves special attention. "There is one body and one Spirit, just as you were called to the one hope that belongs to your call, one Lord, one faith, one baptism, one God and Father of us all, who is above all and through all and in all." This is a glorious hymn specifying the principles of Christian unity. Christians form one body, the Church, anointed by one Spirit and tending towards the same end, heavenly beatitude, the object of their hope. The body finds its unity in the one head, the Lord Jesus, to whom they cling by the same faith and are incorporated by the same baptism. Finally God is the ultimate principle of this unity: he is the Father of all the faithful, lives in all and acts through and in all. "It is in him that we live and move and exist" (Ac 17:28).

In the first century as today there were many recipes and solutions for coming to terms with life. There were a large number of gods and many religious sects or societies through membership of which one's future could be secured, it was thought. But for Paul there is only one solution and one society or body, the Church where the true answer to life is found. In the same way there is only one divine power at work in the world, the Spirit of God. The Christian also has a future, the one hope, the only hope that is valid, certified by the life, death, and resurrection of Jesus Christ. This hope is that God will work his purposes for the world; that nothing at all, including physical death, can separate us from the love of God; and that God has in store for us a full life of fellowship with him. Such hope is purely the result of God's goodness seen in his call to friendship with himself.

In the first century the many cults and mystery religions each had its own head or Lord. But for Paul there is only one Lord Jesus, through whom we are put right with the God of the whole world and gain the only security that matters. This is attained through the one faith, that is, personal allegiance to Jesus, the loyalty that matters. Such faith receives its outward expression in the rite of baptism by which admittance to Christ's family is achieved.

Finally, the unity of the universe is stressed by mention of the one God, in contrast to the belief in many gods, a featuie of the ancient world. But the term Father describes this God as one who is not an abstract principle but as one who has a personal love and care for his world. He is over all as the source of creation, but is through all and in all, as being deeply involved and interested in it.

The Trinitarian character of the passage (Ep 4:4-6) should also be noticed. In this short credal statement the thought begins with the observable Church where God's Spirit is at work, and passes on to the one Lord, the risen Jesus who founded the Church, and through whom the one God and Father of all has been made known.

Intimately related to the Body of Christ theme in Paul's letters is the theme of Christ as *head* of the body which is the Church, a theme that appears early in the Captivity epistles (Col 1:18; Ep 1:23). The head theme appears early in Paul's letters independently of the body theme as a figure of subordination not of unity (e.g., I Cor 11:3-5). But in the captivity epistles the body theme and the head theme are joined and the image is exploited with details from contemporary medical teaching which sees the relation of the head to the human body as a source of life and growth (Ep 4:15-16).

In the epistle to the Colossians head is used of Christ with two connotations: dignity and authority (1:18, 2:10) and source of vitality (2:19). The word head combines the idea of exaltation with that of vital union necessary for an organism. The ascended Christ presides over the Church. He is for it the constant cause and mighty source of spiritual vitality. Its organization grows from him and refers to him.

The name head asserts Christ's inseparability from the Church but excludes identity with it. For all his transcendence Christ is also dependent upon the Church as the head upon the body. In other words the whole Christ is both head and body. Christ is both transcendent (head) and immanent (body).

St. Thomas Aquinas explains the rich analogy of the head as first a pre-eminence of order: as the head dominates the body so Christ occupies the first place in the divine plan of the Church. Also a pre-eminence of perfection: in the head are united all the senses, all the intellectual and appetitive faculties: so in Christ the hypostatic union entails the plenitude of sanctifying grace and of all supernatural gifts. Finally, a pre-eminence of action. The head acts on the body with its thoughts and purposes; as the head moves and rules the body so the members of the mystical body are dependent on Christ, who is their sanctifying and uniting influence. Aquinas also underlines the fact of the community of nature which exists between the head and the body. This in the plan of divine providence is the condition and the starting point of the influence of Christ.

Briefly, this seems to be the Pauline thought on the Body of Christ. It supposes the sacramental union of the bodies of the Christians with Christ's risen body, by faith, baptism, and especially the Eucharist; a consequent building up of a body of Christ, the Church, in constant progress; the government and vivifying of this body by Christ conceived as head, that is, commander-in-chief but also as principle of life; the extension of Christ's influence to the whole cosmos, forming a pleroma of reconciliation and unity; and finally, the plenitude of God himself who in Christ and by Christ is the source and term of this work of recreation (*mirabilius reformasti*). It expresses the basic revelation of Paul's

experience on the road to Damascus: the risen Christ lives in his
own; the eschatological era has begun and since the Christ event
nothing else matters but Christ "who is above all God for ever
blessed" (Rm 9:5), "so that God may be all in all" (I Cor 15:28)
"one God who is Father of all, over all, through all and within
all" (Ep 4:6).

Five

THE EUCHARISTIC MYSTERY

There is always profit in coming back to the Eucharistic mystery in an attempt to assimilate more and better the fruits of this sacred banquet. Eucharistic contemplation is an ever ascending spiral which constantly brings one closer to God as we meditate on the impenetrable heart of the Eucharistic mystery from different angles and viewpoints. Here our approach might be qualified as *pre-scholastic*, namely as an attempt to see the Eucharist exclusively in a traditional biblical perspective.

At its point of origin, the Eucharist appears as the new Paschal meal of God's people, which Christ, having loved his own unto the end, that is, utterly and completely (Jn 13:1), gave them to celebrate in the light of his resurrection until his return in the glory of the Parousia (I Cor 11:17-27). The Last Supper is thus situated at the heart of the Paschal mystery, God's plan for our salvation through the passion, death, and resurrection of our Lord. The mystery of the Eucharist will then be considered in relation to the mystery of the blessed Trinity and the mystery of the Church of which it is the life.

The Eucharist is deeply rooted into the mystery of the blessed Trinity. It reaches each of the divine persons according to each one's personal intervention in the history of our salvation. Since everything comes from the Father and returns to him, the Eucharist is the great thanksgiving to the Father for all he has done in creation and redemption, and for all that he still accomplishes in the Church and in the world. But this thanksgiving can only be addressed to the Father in union with that of Christ in his Paschal mystery. That is why our Lord instituted the Eucharist as the memorial (*anamnesis*) of all his life, especially his death and resurrection. This memorial is not a mere souvenir bringing the Christian community together. In it the risen Christ himself is present and active in the celebration, anticipating and already effecting the coming of God's kingdom. It is a memorial in which Christ works through the joyous celebration of his Church, a representation of his saving work and an anticipation of its blessed consummation.

Gift and memorial of Christ, the Eucharist is also the gift of the Holy Spirit without whose invocation it remains inoperative: "it is the spirit who gives it life" (Jn 6:63). It is the Holy Spirit who, invoked in the assembly and on the bread and wine, renders Christ really present and gives him to us to transform our life. "Let your Spirit come upon these gifts to make them holy, so that they may become for us the body and blood of our Lord Jesus Christ." "May all of us who share in the body and blood of Christ be brought together in unity by the Holy Spirit" (second Eucharistic prayer). In technical terms *anamnesis*, that is the memorial of the Paschal mystery, and *epiclesis*, that is the invocation of the Holy Spirit, are inseparable in the constitution of the Eucharist. Western Latin theology has too long neglected the role of the Holy Spirit in the Eucharistic celebration, yet it is part of a well balanced presentation of the total Eucharistic mystery.

Gift of God, the Eucharist is celebrated by the Church whose life it is. We might recall here the traditional summary of the Eucharistic mystery given by St. Thomas Aquinas in the office for the feast of Corpus Christi. "O sacred banquet in which Christ is received. In it the memory of his passion is renewed, our soul is filled with grace, and we are given a pledge of the glory to come." The ecclesial viewpoint of the Eucharist includes the full panorama of the past, the present, and the future of salvation history. The reference to the past underlines the reality of Christ's presence as memorial of his redemptive passion. Christ gives his body and blood, that is himself, under the signs of bread and wine, himself as he is, that is the Lamb still marked, even in glory, with the signs of his slaughter (Rv 5:6) and always interceding for us (Heb 7:25). That is how in the present the Eucharist is the building up of the Church. By giving himself to those who partake of the sacrament, Christ unites us in the unity of his body. The Church celebrates, makes the Eucharist, but the Eucharist makes the Church, gives it shape and life. It realizes the unity of the communicants with Christ and among themselves, and enables us to work at the union of all men here below. In the Eucharist, the Church joins Christ in his mission of giving himself "for the life of the whole world" (Jn 6:51). Reconciled by the Eucharist, the members of Christ's body become in their turn instruments of reconciliation among men and witnesses of the joy of the resurrection. The sacramental symbolism itself recalls the most concrete consequences of this mission of hope. The Eucharistic celebration is a breaking of bread, the staple of our human life, and a reminder that we cannot in any way give our consent to the condition of our fellow men who are deprived of bread, and are fed with injustice and oppression when they crave for love and peace. This ideal present of the Eucharistic celebration, a soul full of love for God and man orients us to the glorious and final coming of Christ, the eschatological future of all mankind when God shall be all in all (I Cor 15:28), and already makes it a little bit nearer, giving us even now a bit of heaven in hopeful anticipation of the total future fulfillment.

Two essential elements of the Eucharistic mystery deserve special attention: the sacramental sacrifice and the real presence of Christ which is the soul and heart of the Eucharistic celebration.

Speaking of the Eucharistic sacrifice, it is important to affirm the sacrificial character of the Eucharist without prejudice to the unrepeatable uniqueness of the sacrifice of the cross. One must recognize here that some explanations of Catholic theology have been the occasion of a certain ambiguity on this matter, even if the fundamental dogmatic statement involved no such confusion. This affirms clearly the sacrificial dimension of the Eucharist by reference to the unique sacrifice of the cross. The link with Calvary is the sacramental sign, the memorial where the Paschal event is re-presented, that is made present, actualized here and now in its unique reality, in order that the ecclesial people, gathered for the celebration of this memorial, may associate themselves to the sacrifice which Christ offered once and for all to his Father, for us men and for our salvation. The Eucharistic meal is sacrificial because it is the efficacious sign of the gift which Christ makes of himself as bread of life through the sacrifice of his life and death and by his resurrection. It is also the sacrifice of the Church assembled around its Lord, the great sacrifice of praise in which the Church speaks in the name of all creation. This second aspect follows from the first, since it is by celebrating the memorial of the passion, resurrection, and ascension of Christ, our high priest and intercessor, that the Church presents to the Father the unique and perfect sacrifice of his Son and asks God to extend to each of us the benefits of the great work of redemption which it proclaims. In the Eucharist, the Church united with Christ, our redeemer and intercessor, prays for the salvation of the world.

The real presence of Christ in the Eucharist is the heart and the soul of the Eucharistic mystery. It is based on faith in the words of our Lord declaring that he gives us his body to eat and his blood to drink. Christ himself is the basis of our faith in his living and dynamic presence in his sacrament. Christ gives himself in person because of his effective presence in the sacrament. While recognition of the Eucharistic presence is impossible without faith, the presence of Christ to his Church in the Eucharist does not depend on our faith, since it is Christ himself who binds himself by his words and in the Spirit to the sacramental happening which is the sign of his presence. It is of capital importance to understand that the real presence of Christ in the Eucharist does not depend on the subjectivity of the believer; it is an objective presence which results from the will of Christ binding himself to the signs of his presence.

The correct understanding of this objectivity is a delicate matter and precisions on this point are indispensable. It is by the power of Christ's creative word and the operation of the Holy Spirit that bread and wine become a sacrament and consequently "a communion with the body and blood of Christ" (I Cor 10:16), a means of intimate fellowship with Christ. They are henceforth in their ultimate truth, under the external sign, the body and blood of Christ, and remain so in view of their reception. In other words, because of Christ's sovereign intervention and that of his Holy Spirit, the bread and wine are really changed by the power of the primary causality which now gives them existence for a very specific purpose. Both the early Greek and Latin Fathers called this a conversion of the bread and wine to the body and blood of Christ. In fact, the ultimate being of a thing, its basic reality, is what God wants it to be in itself and for us, two aspects which are really inseparable. Now what Christ gives us as his body and blood, in the relation of love which he wants to establish with us, is really his body and blood. If it is so for him and for us, his gift cannot but be so in itself. Such is the foundation and source of the consistency and reality of the Eucharistic gift.

It is useful to recall with St. Thomas Aquinas that the real presence of Christ in the Eucharist "does not mean the localization of Christ in the bread and wine, nor the physico-chemical change of these elements." On the empirical level it is clear that the bread and wine remain bread and wine, and that the Eucharist does not include any technical miracle. It is not on the level of a physico-chemical analysis that is sought the real substance of the bread and wine. According to our traditional Catholic language, this level is that of the appearance of the bread and wine, precisely because of the nature of the sacrament. The miracle of the Eucharist is of another order. The presence of Christ is sacramental, that is, a presence under a sign which does not call for the intervention of secondary causes. It is situated on the level of the first cause; in other words, it is the fruit of the intervention of Christ, the creator, in whom everything subsists; of Christ re-creator who in virtue of his sovereign power as risen Lord controls the whole universe, and has liberated his own body from the finite, and exercises his omnipotence by the gift of his Holy Spirit. The link between the real presence of the body of Christ in the Eucharist and the glorious body of our risen Lord would be a fruitful source for theological reflection.

The sacramental presence of Christ in the Eucharist of its nature is permanent until the consumption of the sacrament or the disappearance of the sacramental elements through other natural causes. What Christ gives as his body and blood remains his body and blood and must be recognized and treated as such (I Cor 12: 29-30). The gift of Christ is irreversible; our earthly bread and wine have been introduced by the Eucharistic happening into the history of salvation. Nothing can withdraw them from the reality of this history which God writes for us in Christ, his Word. As long as they are present as signs of bread and wine, they remain the sign of the loving presence of Christ who gives himself as our food and drink.

Such is our Christian faith manifested in the most ancient tradition. St. Justin, in the middle of the second century attests that the Eucharist was brought to the absent and the sick after the church celebration. Tertullian in the third century states that the early Christians could bring the Eucharist home, after the Sunday celebration, to communicate during the week. The custom of reserving the sacrament with time was richly amplified, the presence of Christ being treated with due respect, adoration, and worship under different forms. It is true that at first the specific purpose of the Eucharistic reserve was not directly adoration, but reverence was always implicit, and it was normal and natural that with time one would adore precisely because the sacrament was reserved. This expansion of Eucharistic worship outside the Mass is perfectly legitimate, even if it has not been universal in the Church. The Orthodox churches, for example, reserve the Eucharist, but in the sacristy and do not present it for the adoration of the faithful. Yet it is also true that specific Eucharistic devotion is not lacking in those churches; the fact is that the length of their actual celebrations is due to the worship of our Eucharistic Lord in hymns and prayers.

Christ remains in the sacrament, and adoration of the blessed Sacrament should be seen in the context of the dynamism of the sacrament in which Christ gives himself. It focuses on the moment of the Eucharistic celebration which extends from the Eucharistic prayer to the actual reception of Holy Communion. Veneration of Christ present in the Eucharist is based on the fact that his presence is the soul of the sacrifice and is meant to foster our life of union with God by Holy Communion.

A word might be added about the minister of the Eucharist.

It is Christ who presides at his Supper as host, and gives himself to us who are his guests. His presidency is signified by the sacramental priesthood of a minister whom he has called and sent. This ministry shows that the assembly is not the proprietor of the action it is performing in the Eucharistic celebration, but that it receives it from Christ himself living in his Church. The priestly mission finds its origin and its norm in that of the Apostles; it is transmitted in the Church by the imposition of hands and the invocation of the Holy Spirit. This transmission insures the continuity of the ministerial charge which evidently also demands fidelity to apostolic teaching and a life conforming to the gospel pattern. Hence our communion prayer: "Keep me faithful to your teaching."

Finally, the mystery of the Eucharist can be summarized briefly according to Incarnational theology which focuses on salvation history on God's plan for our salvation through Christ's redemptive Incarnation. This involved the assumption of a human body, a body which was crucified and rose again, a body which is made available to us all in the Eucharist to build up the mystical body, the Church. From the liturgical viewpoint which focuses on sacramental notions, the Eucharistic mystery appears again in a wonderful light. Christ is the sacrament of our encounter with God; the Church is the sacrament of Christ; and we Christians should be the sacrament both of Christ and of his Church.

Six

THE MYSTERY OF CHRIST'S EUCHARISTIC PRESENCE

The mystery of Christ's presence in the Eucharist cannot be given a total and complete explanation precisely because it is a supernatural truth, a fact that is beyond human comprehension. Our human reason already partially loses its grasp in the natural mystery of what substance is in the natural order, and we are completely routed and lost by the idea of what sacrament means in the supernatural order.

The real presence is beyond the reach of our experience of the physical world or any possibility of sensible control. The mystery is beyond philosophical speculation, logic, and the knowledge acquired by sensible experience.

Christ is present in the Eucharist "by a mode of existence which we cannot express in words, but which with a mind illumined by faith, we can conceive, and must firmly believe to be possible to God" (*Mysterium Fidei*).

According to the Council of Trent, Christ is present in heaven according to his natural way of existing. He is present to us in the Eucharist sacramentally, in his own complete being, truly, really, and substantially.

The catechism of the Council of Trent explains that the true body of Christ, the Lord, the same that was born of the Virgin and is now seated at the right hand of the Father, is contained in this sacrament.

In this sacrament are contained not only the true body of Christ and all the constituents of a true body such as bones and sinews but also Christ whole and entire. The word Christ designates the God-man, that is to say, one Person in whom are united

the divine and human natures. The Holy Eucharist therefore contains both natures and whatever is included in the idea of both,
the divinity and the humanity whole and entire consisting of the
soul, all the parts of the body and the blood. In heaven the whole
humanity is united to the divinity in one hypostasis or Person.
Now when two things are actually united, where one is the other
also must be. So far the catechism of Trent.

Without denying that Christ is present in the Eucharist as the
signified in the sign, or as the reality under a figure, or by the
virtue of the sacrament as the divine power in its instrument,
Christ's Eucharistic presence is not sufficiently explained by these
minimal concepts. There is more here than a mere sign, or symbol,
or pure dynamism. Christ is signified as truly, really, and substantially present. This is a categorical statement, clear and simple,
affirming without any restriction the real presence of the very
reality and truth of the nature and substance of Christ's body and
blood.

Truly : since the terms "This is my body" are not used in an
improper or metaphorical sense. *Really :* stresses the absence of
figure as found in such expressions as "Christ was the rock" (I Cor
10:4; Jn 10:7, 15:1). *Substantially :* because what is present is the
very being of Christ, human and divine, not only his divine power
of sanctification.

Christ since his resurrection is glorious and immortal, eternally
living in the integrity of his two natures and the indivisible unity
of his person; he is entirely present where there is any part of his
being. The Eucharist consequently contains the body and blood
of the living Christ, that is, all his human nature which is inseparably united to the divine nature in the unity of his person, and
hence the whole Christ, body, blood, soul, and divinity is present
under the consecrated species, by virtue of what has been called
the law of concomitance or coexistence.

The manner of the presence of Christ's body in the Eucharist
is not that in which a body is present in a place. This quantitative
and local presence is proper to his presence in heaven, that mysterious and unimaginable place which is the abode of the elect.
The Eucharistic presence of Christ's body is rather after the man-

ner in which a spirit is present all in the whole being and all in any of its parts. Yet with this difference that Christ's body, contrary to what is usual for a substance, is also present elsewhere.

St. Thomas' explanation of this phenomenon is noteworthy. If fire is to be in a place, I can bring it there from a point where it already was, but I can also light wood present here and now and transform it into fire. What I cannot do is to transform it into a fire existing elsewhere and continuing to exist there. But our Lord can make himself present in the Eucharist without interfering with his actual presence in heaven.

Another simple comparison might also be helpful. A mother could have simultaneously two ways of being corporally present: one manifest for her clear-eyed child, another real but hidden from her other child who is blind.

The real presence is not an empty word, a superstition, or an imaginary myth, but a sacred reality. The Eucharistic mystery creates a presence in time, first of all, between the past of the cross and the future of heavenly glory. A presence in space also, that is, a presence perceptible to our bodily senses.

The real presence is not to be understood as a localization of Christ which would limit his presence exclusively to the elements of bread and wine. But the species do become a privileged place where Christ himself in his humanity and deity may be met and received corporally. They are a concrete sign of his presence, a place where he may be found locally, contemplated sensibly, and communicated concretely. The Church knows that Christ is there objectively and it receives him by means of a concrete sign.

There is no physical or chemical transformation of the species yet by the empirical being of bread it is no longer with bread that we are dealing but with the body of Christ. The material bread has become the bread of life (Jn 6:57-58).

The supernatural realism of the real is stressed in *Mysterium Fidei*. After the consecration the species "contain a new reality which we may justly term ontological. Christ whole and entire in his physical reality is bodily present."

The Eucharistic change is ontological, total, intrinsic, metaphysical, because it affects the food-turned-person in the depths of its being. The purpose of the bread and wine had originally been to nourish physically. Now these elements put the recipient in personal contact with Christ through his new presence. The bread and wine before consecration signified ordinary eating, the strength food gives and the fellowship of a meal. After transubstantiation the species signify and effect the new life given by the glorified Christ to those who accept him in faith. The consecrated species have a new finality and a superior signification precisely because they are consecrated and have a new ontological reality.

We find in the Eucharist a wonderful blend of realism and symbolism: a real and corporal presence of the glorious Christ in all that constitutes his personality including his body, but a presence that is not spatial or carnal but sacramental, that is, effected by the sign of the sacrament. And Christ's gift involves him personally in all that he is and till the end of time (I Cor 11:26).

The ontological reality of the Eucharist, in fact, is essentially *personal* since it is the real presence of the person of our Lord. This is clearly stated in Scripture: the words of consecration mean, I give myself to you, all that I am. It is I personally, Jesus the Son of God (I Cor 11:27). And Trent has explained that this person is present as Incarnational (the divinity being essentially united to Christ's body, blood, and soul) not just in power or spirit.

Our Christian religion is essentially personalist in character. It is the service and adoration of a person, religion of the presence of the Son of God, incarnate, dead, and risen from the dead. Adherence to Christianity is attachment to the person of Christ, a person now glorious by the consummation of his sacrifice, yet sacramentally available to all the Christian people in the Eucharist.

Our Lord wants to be our sacrifice and sacrament, our priest and our victim, and he does so personally and not in mere sign or figure or vicariously.

An essential element in the Eucharist is not verified in the analogy suggested by the elements of the sacrament. Material nourishment easily puts into mind the idea of spiritual nourishment but gives no hint of the personal encounter which is essential in the Eucharist.

The body and blood of Christ are present in the Eucharist but not statically, passively, or inactively. The Eucharist is not only a mystery, it is also a personal action of Christ. It is not merely an encounter of the human mind and heart with an abstract idea but a personal encounter, an act of communion which applies Christ's redemption to men.

Holy Communion is a union of persons, a dialogue between Christ and the Christian, a harmonious cooperation, ultimately a belonging to the person of Christ, even a spiritual oneness (Jn 6:57) between him and the faithful. Briefly, the Eucharist is the most deeply personal experience possible with Christ.

In every sacrament Christ acts and gives himself, but this personal action and gift is realized eminently in the Eucharist. The blood of the covenant of which we partake in the Eucharistic cup saves us because of him who shed it and gave himself completely and forever on the Cross and renews this gift personally in the Eucharist.

The supreme mark or token of love is the absolute gift of one's body: witness marriage and voluntary vicarious death (Jn 15:13). In the Eucharist Christ proclaims (I Cor 11:26), makes actual the Paschal event, the New Covenant, by the permanent gift he makes of all himself to his Father and to the Church as a center of unity and salvation.

One may be present to someone-else in thought or desire, for example by sending greetings. Or again a validating document such as an affidavit or last testament represents a personal action in absentia. To be really present personally is to actually exist for someone near him and with him, and this is the personal way in which our Lord gives himself to us in the Eucharist.

The mystery of the Incarnation consisted in the personal assumption of a human nature by the Son of God to unite the family of men to the divinity, the divine family. The Eucharist is the actual and practical realization of this objective of the Incarnation. It is a power that elevates the human community to the very heart of the Trinity.

The Eucharist is the presence of Christ's divine Person which is essentially incarnated. And just as it was by his flesh that the Son was incarnated, so also it is by his flesh that he becomes present and unites us to himself in Holy Communion. The Incarnation was the supreme model of adaptation; Christ became like us (Heb 4:15) in order to win us over and save us. The principle is carried to its full application in the Eucharist where by nourishing ourselves with his flesh and blood we are built up into the perfection of his Mystical Body, and our very body will ultimately share in the glory of his risen body (Jn 6:54).

The Eucharist is not only the extension of the Incarnation but also of Christ's redemption which like and with the Eucharist was the immolation of his flesh for the life of the world (Jn 6:51). The Eucharistic presence is not only incarnational but also redemptive, victimal, sacrificial. The flesh of the Word Incarnate is flesh that has been immolated and in the Eucharist Christ gives himself as our victim and our priest. The Christian who would forget this aspect of the real presence would miss the fundamental meaning of the mystery.

Christ is present in the Eucharist as our immolated victim, yet his Eucharistic body is living and life-giving, even glorious. Mass is not a funeral, a burial service but a work of life, an Easter celebration. It commemorates the death of Jesus and renews his sacrifice in order to communicate to us the triumphant life of the Resurrection.

The Eucharistic body of Christ is the divinized and vivifying body of the Incarnate Word, who wants to vivify and divinize the Christian. It is the body of the resurrected Christ, the focal point of vital communion of life between God and man (Jn 6:57). By the Eucharist the faithful is gradually assimilated to Christ's Mystical Body, the Church, and strengthens his communion with the Father and with his brethren. The Church on earth, the earthly Jerusalem is thus constantly moving closer to the heavenly Jerusalem described in the Apocalypse.

The modern stress on the personalist presence of Christ in the Eucharist is very rewarding. Such a presence is established by the communication of one person with another; it is activity, presence of mind and heart, love in action that is communication and communion. It is based on personal relation, active communion.

When I make myself present to someone there can be degrees. Presence can be more or less intense according to the intensity of my personal activity, my giving. This presence would be complete if the giving of myself could be complete.

In this perspective we find the principle for the integration, the harmonious co-ordination of the different real presences of our Lord to the Christian people. Christ already communicates himself to us in the liturgy of the word because he actually addresses his word to us. This is wonderful but there is more. The supreme sign of love, sacrifice, his complete gift of himself is signified effectively in the sacrament. This sign of redemptive love is a gesture, a dynamic reality, a real presence which achieves redemption for us, as well as the greatest glory for the Father. This is no inert, static presence like that of an object in a given place: in the Eucharist Christ is truly present because he gives himself completely to his Father and to men.

By the consecration Christ becomes present not as if manifesting himself for the first time and to strangers, becoming suddenly present where he was totally absent before. Christ is present already in the hearts of Christians by faith, speaking inwardly, invisibly, silently in the depths of our heart through the Holy Spirit (Rm 5:5). He is present in a special way when Christians assemble in his name (Mt 18:20), especially for the liturgy. He is present in his priests through the sacerdotal character.

At the consecration and communion Christ's presence in word, in power, and in spirit is intensified and his new presence surpasses all that we can imagine, just as the idea of a glorified body, the reality of the risen Christ, is far beyond our understanding. It is the real presence par excellence because Christ gives himself completely, showing the greatest love for his Father and for men, his brethren. The Eucharistic gift is an act which summarizes all his life, recapitulates the whole history of salvation and brings it to its final fulfillment.

Seven

THE EUCHARISTIC MYSTERY IN
SALVATION HISTORY

The total Eucharistic revelation is given summarily in Jn 6:51, "The bread that I shall give is my flesh for the life of the world." The Eucharist is the personal gift our Savior makes of himself for our salvation, which includes our ultimate glorification (54).

The Eucharistic mystery is closely knit into the mystery of the Incarnation and of the Redemption. Man lives on the Word made flesh (Jn 6:51, 57). Jesus is our true bread as God's Word of revelation to man (32-33) and as the victim offered in sacrifice for the salvation of the world (51-58). The only true life available is by our assimilation of the Eucharistic mystery (57).

The basic scriptural and theological notion is that the Eucharist is food. It is the sacrament of Christ who, as our Redeemer, gives himself as food to men to transform us into himself and constitute, build up his Mystical Body which is the Church; a gift which reproduces and applies in an unbloody manner the sacrifice of the Cross.

The immediate purpose of the Eucharistic presence is union with Christ and his Church, but Christ is present above all as priest and victim, with all that these concepts imply, especially his eternal priesthood. The Eucharist is a sacrifice as well as a sacrament. It was instituted to announce the death of Christ (1 Cor 11:26), to memorialize effectively what Christ has done for our salvation.

Just as the Incarnation was essentially redemptive, so also Communion is a participation in Christ's sacrifice, and Christ present in the Eucharist is the immolated Christ (Rv 5:6), the same who died for us and will raise us up and glorify us one day.

In the Eucharist the redemptive work of Christ is contained, manifested, and made effective. The sacrament manifests the sacrifice; the sacrifice is sacramental. And Christ, the real presence of his body and blood, is the primordial, the fundamental reality of the Mass. The sacrifice of the Mass depends essentially on the presence of Christ. The Mass is Christ giving himself again invisibly but really to his Father and to his Church and the faithful.

What Christ affirms absolutely in the Eucharist is his presence. This is the basic reality on which all other Eucharistic values are built. All the efficacy of Mass and Communion derive from the presence of Christ, our only (1 Tm 2:5) and eternal priest (Heb 7:24). There would be no Mass without the presence of him who is the priest and victim of his sacrifice and ours.

It is not really the meal or sacrifice which give sense to Christ's Eucharistic presence; it is rather his presence which gives meaning and value to both, and must be recognized (1 Cor 11:29) by the faithful if the sacrament is to have its salutary effect.

Medieval theologians have concentrated on the real presence as such and for them the great problem was how Christ's natural and historical body is identical yet different from his Eucharistic body. Today transubstantiation with all its technical problems monopolizes practically all the attention of the modern theological authors. These questions are important but that is not all that is involved in the Eucharist. The Eucharistic mystery must also be situated exactly in the history of our salvation, in time and eternity, but especially in consideration of the very essence of God's saving plan.

The full content of the Eucharistic mystery may be stated first in relation to time which in our viewpoint is the duration of salvation history. Thus in relation to the past, the Eucharist is a commemoration, a memorial which makes present and renews the sacrifice of the Cross. In relation to the present, the Eucharist is a gift and token of love provoking our loving adoration and our grateful love, a communion by which the unity of the Church is effected. In relation to the future, the consummation of all the faithful in glory, the Eucharist is the prefiguration and anticipation of our beatifying union with God. The Eucharistic presence is the tangent between heaven and earth, the true Jacob's ladder, the point of contact at which our terrestrial reality touches its eschatological fulfillment.

The mode of Christ's presence is thus intermediary in character. Christ in this sacrament is not present with the mode of his past natural and historical being, nor with the mode which is proper to his natural being as transformed in glory. The Eucharistic presence participates of both and makes us pass from one to the other. By it we already enter in a mysterious way in the eschatological present, enjoying an actual moment of realized salvation in which we truly share. This eschatological present in which past and future meet is as yet fully realized only in the glorified Christ and in his mother by virtue of the privilege of the Assumption.

Christ in the Eucharist is present in a way which is the living synthesis of revelation. The Eucharist is a recapitulation of Christ's saving mission, its complete fulfillment. His presence is a flash-back on the past, being the memorial of his passion and death. It is also a contact, an encounter in spirit and in truth with the risen and living Lord, a gift of love to enkindle our own, and vivify his Mystical Body. Finally, it is also an invasion, an eruption in our world by the final reality, veiled but accessible to our faith, the beginning of the new heaven and the new world (Rv 21:5). The Eucharistic presence is thus the meeting of heaven and earth where Christ presents himself for our contemplation and assimilation, as the supreme reality, past, present and future.

Vatican II (SC) puts it this way: the Eucharist is "a memorial of Christ's death and resurrection, a sacrament of love, a sign of unity, a bond of charity, a paschal banquet in which Christ is received, the mind is filled with grace, and a pledge of future glory is given to us" (no. 47).

The Eucharist is that sacrament which as the effective memorial of Christ's saving death and resurrection is the covenant—sacrifice—meal of the new people of God, recalling the covenant's sealing on Calvary, actualizing the covenant union in the worshipping assembly in so far as they cooperate in faith and charity, and anticipating the covenant's perfect fulfillment in the eschatological Messianic banquet (Rv 19:9).

The relations of Christ with us by the Eucharist are not in line with his natural and historical existence, as if the Eucharist were Christ's natural life continued after death. The presence of Jesus in the tabernacle is not the continuation of his historical life; it is intrinsically conditioned by his death and resurrection.

The Eucharistic mystery, in fact, plunges its roots deeply into God's saving plan, salvation history, God's purpose of uniting Himself to all men by means of the Incarnation and the Passion. This redemptive Incarnation is described by St. Paul (Ph 2:6-11) as a kenotic (self-emptying) action by which the Son of God became man and accepted to be reduced to the condition of a slave. Jesus thus became present in the world, went about doing good (Ac 10:38), but above all sacrificed his life on the cross, ratifying and consummating the gift of himself to men as their food at the Last Supper to unite them in the community of his own Mystical Body. All Christ's relations with men in their world and their history are thus gathered together, and are signified and effected by his presence in the Eucharist.

This concept of presence needs further elucidation especially to understand the spiritual relations the Eucharistic presence established with men to whom Christ gives himself to form his Mystical Body. The notion of presence has two dimensions: it can be considered *in itself*, a viewpoint which specifies also what the being does for itself; presence must also be examined in relation *to other* beings. Now a personal presence, as opposed to a purely local presence, implies evidently the presence in itself, the actual real presence, of the one who is present, yet it includes also essentially the relations established with others, communication by word and action, a more or less extensive gift of self.

Scholastic theology interested in ontology tends to neglect these relations which are labeled as accidents with the danger of the substance becoming some kind of degraded, stripped thing, albeit glorified with a transcendental sense. Modern analytics, on the contrary, focuses on personal relations practically all its attention, sometimes refusing to pronounce itself on ontological values or finding in them little or no interest.

Looking at Christ's Eucharistic presence, the concept of substantial presence stresses the fact of Christ's presence as such, considered in itself; thus, if it abstracts from the relational concept, especially the relation to us men, the concept of presence will be impoverished to a mere local presence, some kind of more or less inert being there or static presence. Christ's substantial presence should reveal all its personal and spiritual character by being thought of from the relational viewpoint. The two aspects should really not be separated but considered in their natural unity.

The life of our Lord, his death and resurrection unfold the different moments or stages of what could be called his total presence in our human history. There was a first time when the personal and spiritual presence, his life with the relations it established with other human beings, was immediately one with the being who was there in the spatio-temporal world of nature and history. This was the case of our Lord living with his disciples among the Jews in Palestine. In this first stage there was no problem, in a sense, because the relations of person to person and the actual being were there together. Yet there was a problem in the fact that the personal relations could be spoiled by a superficial approach to the presence. Jesus was there but that did not dispense people from knowing him more or less in depth as a person. This is one of the reasons why he said one day: "It is to your advantage that I go away" (Jn 16:7).

There comes, in fact, a second stage in personal relations when the being there, the physical presence, can be withdrawn. The personal and spiritual presence must then affirm itself, at least for those who are faithful to the memory of the absent or departed one, and it is deepened not in contrast to the being in itself but to the being as locally present. This is the time when human relations are strengthened, when a friend discovers that he is with his friend even if the loved one is not physically present, when deep faith and true love are developed. It was the time when the Apostles and the primitive Church were deprived of the local presence of Jesus, but not of his personal and spiritual presence. It is the time of Christ's spiritual presence among his own (Mt 28:20), assisting and governing invisibly his Church, reigning over consciences, and of his presence when the community assembles (Mt 18:20) for common prayer or for the celebration of the Eucharist.

But there is still a third moment when this general and constant presence of Christ in his Church is surpassed and perfected. Then the personal and spiritual presence is not reached only by the intermediary of the faith of the believer, or of his memory, or by some exterior sign (as a relic, or Holy Scripture) but is again one with the being itself, no longer as in the first state, but in the consummation of Christ's saving work. The local presence which in the first stage was all material is now elevated to the rich interiority of the personal and spiritual presence in a perfect synthesis.

Such is for the elect Christ's presence in heaven. Such was to a lesser degree the presence of Christ to his apostles in the repeated apparitions after his resurrection, and such finally is the Eucharistic presence under the transparent sacramental sign, for the pure faith of the assembled Church.

Christ's presence as such and the relations it establishes are realities that are intimately connected and should really not be separated. Without the spatio-temporal presence of Christ in the natural and human world, there would be no kenosis, evangelical preaching, or sacrifice on the cross. So also without the substantial presence of Christ in the Eucharist there would be no total gift of himself as food, uniting and sustaining the Mystical Body, renewing the mystery of our redemption, and fulfilling the grace of our salvation.

Salvation history could have been worked out in a number of other ways, but this is the one the wonderful counsel of God's providence has chosen and effected.

Eight

THE EUCHARIST TODAY

During the last decade Eucharistic theology and devotion have taken important new orientations. There is first of all in the Church today a revaluation of the Word of God in the Bible and, consequently, a better balance between Word and Sacrament. A fruit of the biblical and liturgical movements, this development is consecrated in many conciliar texts where the *Two Tables*, the Bible and the Eucharist are equally prominent (e.g., DV, nos. 21, 26) and where strong emphasis is placed on the ministry of evangelization confided to bishops and priests (LG, ch. 3).

The Council presents clearly the Gospel as the *foundation* of the life of the Church, yet the Eucharist is just as clearly pointed out as its *center and summit* (LG, no. 11; PO, no. 6). Notice, however, that today at the council or elsewhere, when a theologian speaks of the Eucharist what he has in mind, first and above all, is the Eucharistic action, the sacrificial meal in which Christ gathers to himself his Church, unites it to his unique sacrifice by giving it his body and blood as food.

The Mass is seen as a *sacramental* sacrifice. It is not a new immolation of Jesus Christ who died and rose again once and for all, but a presence of the immolation of the Cross by means of a significant rite, one that effects what it signifies.

The Eucharist is necessarily the sacramental presence of Christ as priest and victim under the appearances of bread and wine. This presence lasts as long as the sacramental signs. Of this there can be no doubt, just as it is always true that where Christ is present, he deserves our adoration. But there is hardly anyone today for whom the Mass is primarily the means of perpetuating the sacramental presence. The reservation of the Eucharist is seen more exactly as the extension of the grace of the Mass, as the banquet always available especially for the sick. Recentered on Mass and Communion, piety is not so attached to rites of substitution like the Benedictions with the Blessed Sacrament.

Then, the Mass is a *community* act. At the Eucharistic celebration Christ and his Church exchange the mutual gift of themselves to glorify the Father. Now for the Church, the gift of self to Christ means union with the worship of her spouse, but also missionary work for the salvation of the whole world. In order that God may be all in all (1 Cor 15:28) Christ died and rose again, sending his Church to all the ways and byways. At Mass the Christian community commits itself to work for the inclusion of all human and cosmic reality in the homage of the total Christ, Jesus and his Mystical Body, to God the Father.

And so the true meaning of the Church emerges from the Eucharistic celebration. The people of God can no longer be simple spectators or recipients; they become actors involved in the work of the Church.

The ministerial priesthood is not thereby eclipsed. It is better situated as an instrument of Christ, the Head, associating his Mystical Body to his sacrifice. The priestly *power* remains but integrated in a ministry, a function of *service*.

Finally, by undertaking the direction of the pilgrim Church, the purpose of its earthly journey, the Council focused attention on the prefigurative and premonitory character of the Eucharist. The sacramental banquet sketches and announces the eschatological banquet, the eternal feast, the gathering of all God's children in the heavenly Jerusalem around Christ manifested in all his glory.

Much is being written today about the Eucharist as a sacrificial *memorial*. It can be discussed whether or not the Last Supper was actually a Paschal meal; in any case, there is no doubt that, like the passion of Christ, it took place during the Paschal octave celebration and that its atmosphere, structure, and signification are Paschal. Like the Jewish Passover, the Eucharist is a memorial of salvation.

The biblical memorial is not only an occasion to recall subjectively a souvenir. It is a *community* rite referring to the covenant of God, recalling the accomplished salvation, and announcing the total definitive salvation yet to come. It is not merely the awakening of a souvenir or a hope; it is a presence of salvation given today with reference to past historical manifestations as well as to the eschatological future.

Such a vital density for the rite is clearly not simply the result of human initiative. God himself prescribed it, ordered it repeated, and so has personally committed in each celebration his permanent power and constant fidelity. Thus the essential element of salvation is made present as the ritual recalls the manifestations of yesterday and already unveils the glory of the future.

This is how the Eucharist is the memorial of the true and definitive *redemptive* act of Calvary. It places us in the presence of our salvation, of Christ giving himself in his passage from this world to his Father and ordering his disciples to repeat this memorial, a recall of the Paschal gift already accomplished, and an announcement of the Parousia, the total eschatological gift. Every time we eat this bread and drink the cup we proclaim the death of the Lord until he comes (1 Cor 11:26).

The Eucharistic action has an ascending and a descending movement. Jesus accepted his death in filial obedience to his Father and out of redemptive love for us. The object of his mission is the kingdom of God, that is, God's sovereignty over us. As St. Irenaeus puts it: "the living man is the glory of God, and the life of man is the vision of God."

Just as the sin of the first Adam involves us all who have ratified it hundreds of times by our personal sins, so also the sacrifice of the second Adam involves all of us and we ratify it every time that our liberty commits itself to the charity of Christ, according to the demands of faith and the thrust of hope.

Offering himself, Christ offered us in advance. By saying our Amen of faith, we consent to his offering, the offering he makes of himself and of us in him; we subscribe personally, under the impulse of the Holy Spirit, to the total sacrifice of which Christ, as our head, is the priest and victim.

There are many Masses but only one sacrifice, that of the

Cross. Masses are not an addition to the unique and definitive sacrifice any more than bank notes, certificates give value to the gold deposit they represent. The Mass is not a sacrifice by itself, it is a sacramental sacrifice. It is the memorial of the unique sacrifice, the manifested and operative actuality of this sacrifice.

It follows that the Mass has no effects proper to itself. Its effects are uniquely and integrally those of the sacrifice of Jesus Christ being made operative in our time. The Mass is the homage of Christ on the Cross to his Father, Christ as head of the Church today, associating the Church to his adoration, his love, and his thanksgiving. The Mass is the supplication of the eternal high Priest for today's Church and today's world, a prayer to which we are united in the Holy Spirit. The Mass is also for all sinners, living and dead, the propitiatory sacrifice of the Cross actually offered by the whole Christ, and operative for those who accept it.

This offering of the Church at Mass might seem like a rather ambiguous, sentimental gesture. Such it might be if man were its source, but this is not the case. The Christian sacrifice has only one source, God made man, and it is from the heart of Christ that its salutary influence reaches our own heart by loving faith and in the Holy Spirit.

In actual reality this salutary influence seems identified with what Scripture, followed by tradition and the recent Council, calls *spiritual sacrifices*. All the life of the Church, as orientated and animated by faith and its mission, is charity translated into action. And this active charity is the true reality of each Eucharistic celebration as the sacrifice of the body united to Christ its head.

The Eucharistic action, memorial sacrifice of the new Adam (man), may then be given this descriptive but complete definition. It is the ritual act of the High Priest, Jesus Christ, by his ecclesial body, prolonging and actualizing each day the Paschal mystery, the unique and total sacrifice; preparing the eschatological recapitulation when God will be all in all; and finding an expression of his own charity, in homage to the Father, in the spiritual sacrifices of the faithful; and all this in a full human context. The Eucharist is the sacramental relay between the unique priesthood of Christ and the earthly life of his disciples.

This is true of the Church as a whole and of each individual member in proportion to his real commitment to the mission of the Church and in proportion to his participation in the actual Eucharistic celebration. Communion, the best participation is the particularization, the personal appropriation of the Mass. And since "at each celebration of this commemorative offering the work of our redemption is accomplished" (repeated several times at the Council) the one who communicates well, receives the personal gift of Christ who died and rose again: a human-divine presence which sanctifies him, confirms his intention of serving God and his brethren in his moral and practical life and in his apostolate. At the same time, it purifies him of his past sins, gives him more liberty from his evil inclinations, and prepares him for the glorious resurrection.

Jesus Christ cannot *give himself* to us and to the Father if he is not present to us by the signs of his gift. The Eucharistic action cannot really be a memorial of the redemptive gift, if the Redeemer does not give himself really, if he is not really present. This is the nerve center of all the doctrine of the Eucharistic presence and of transubstantiation.

To understand the teaching of the Church and its full validity, we start again from the redemptive act of which the Eucharist is the memorial: in his Paschal mystery Christ gives himself to us in his Father's name, and to his Father in our name. He gives his body and blood inseparably.

The *body* is the person itself as expressed in the world and in history, as present to other persons and communicating with them. By giving his body to the Church the risen Christ gathers God's people together, and with a certitude grounded on his victory over death and on his divinity, he communicates his Holy Spirit, the principle of eternal life, and joy of all apostolic activity.

The *blood* is the person as immolated in sacrifice, the cross realizing definitely what the Jewish sacrifices prefigure, sacrifices in which the role of blood was preponderant.

The Eucharist cannot then be truly the memorial of Christ's death and resurrection unless Jesus in this sacrament gives himself to his Church, here and now, as vivifying and unifying body and as sacrificial blood.

In the Eucharistic memorial we consequently receive *today* the body and blood of Christ, who gave himself once and for all to God and to the Church, his spouse, by his death and resurrection. It is today that the Church of today receives this gift of himself from her spouse. Without this actual gift the Church could not survive, it would cease to be, it would die of inanition.

By means of his priest, Christ gives himself. The Eucharistic signs effect what they signify, namely, the gift of Christ's redemptive body and blood. And if they are really given they are really present.

The Church exists only as the Body of Christ, her spouse. Her privileged status is not due to the merits of her members but purely to the grace of God. Jesus Christ untiringly gives himself to her and takes her to himself in the Spirit, by means of the Eucharistic memorial and all the other sacraments that gravitate around the Eucharist as their sun of life.

Nine

THE LITURGICAL RENEWAL

Among all the points of discussion, tension, and even opposition encountered in our post-Vatican II Church, two stand out prominently, the priest and the Mass, and are closely related.

Formerly the parochial community was stability itself, and a pastor could gauge the state of his parish by keeping track of Easter communions. Today more and more people choose the church they go to. Some do so for practical reasons, like the Mass schedules or the parking facilities; or esthetical reasons like church architecture or decoration; others for more valid reasons like the style of celebration, facility of participation, or even the priest's homiletic ability.

Most of our people, however, cannot and do not stray from their local church, yet they are constantly faced with all sorts of disturbing questions and problems. Troubled by constant experimentation and changes many ask themselves whether the vaunted community participation in the Eucharistic celebration is not destroying the pattern of personal, private prayer. Is the new order of the Mass truly a step forward or a stalemate in a liturgical morass? Should we rejoice because of the possibilities of adaptation and experimentation, or find in them the seeds of anarchy? Are group Masses (where just a few people gather, people who know each other and have similar objectives) really a step towards a more authentic celebration, or just a fragmentation of the community? Must we at all costs preserve a certain cultural patrimony or do we have the audacity and imagination necessary to baptize other cultures and approaches, as our predecessors have done?

Whether our new liturgical possibilities are considered risks or opportunities will depend on our individual mentality, sensibilities, or even prejudices. Yet the out-and-out imprudence of some will become a pretext for others to harden their conservatism; while routine enshrined as a principle might be the occasion for the contrary tendency to put everything into question. Reforms should not compromise the faith of God's people, a faith which is very closely related to the expression of God's mysteries in actual rites. A sufficient catechesis should precede any ritual change, otherwise there is a risk of just replacing one meaningless gimmick with another.

We must respect other people's faith-attitude in trying to instruct and to lead them on in their faith. Actually, most people are happy to pray in their own language and to understand what the priest at Mass tells the congregation or asks God in their name; or to participate in the celebration by singing, responding, and in all cases knowing what is going on. Christian faith is rich in good will, generosity, and submission to the Church, when it is properly directed and encouraged, according to the old liturgical adage that faith and prayer walk hand in hand (*lex orandi, lex credendi*).

The post-Vatican II renewal of the Mass emphasizes its essential character as an assembly of God's people. Everyone is invited to cooperate, to express himself and identify himself with the celebration; to sing together, dialogue with the celebrant, and take part in the different ceremonies. The celebrant ceases to be the one man orchestra of former days and associates each and everyone of the faithful, as much as possible, to his priestly action. Discarded or at least discredited are the simple looking on of the spectator who refuses to get involved, or the rugged individualism of the person busy in irrelevant activities (lighting votive candles!), but also the free-for-all confusion where anyone would intervene with anything at any time (for example, spontaneous dances, clapping of hands, or other emotional outbursts). A reverent celebration demands respect for the different ministers and ministries, a co-ordination of everyone's activities, a logic of accord between all the actions, words, and songs, a human and ecclesial interaction between the altar and the people to promote the growth of Christ's mystical body.

Singing along might not be as artistic as the rendition of difficult, choice pieces by a glorious choir, yet it surely is the best realization of the original purpose of our grand organs. And when all is said and done, one way of doing need not exclude another. It surely is a shame that our choirs especially the *scholae* of Gregorian chant (remember when this church song was the trademark of genuine liturgy?), have practically disappeared under the pretext of hearing from the congregation. A choir or even a soloist could help the tempo of a good celebration. Everybody need not sing everything. Here again, good common sense, the little brother of the inspiring Spirit, will suggest good solutions within the possibilities of the audience. Better a careful proclamation or musical rendition than a blaring organ or vocal song leader with practically no response from the congregation, whatever the cause of this community failure. The possibility of choice allows for and even suggests that an effort should be made toward both perfection and artistic education.

Is it less true today that the liturgy is the best Church school, the best catechetical instrument the Church has at its disposal? In many iron or bamboo curtain countries the liturgy, when available, is practically the only source of spiritual nourishment. And for other reasons, the same is perhaps true for the great majority of practicing Christians elsewhere, who have little contact with their Church except through weekly or occasional attendance at the Eucharistic celebration. In these conditions the renewed emphasis on the liturgy of the word meets an evident need. Hence the primary importance given to it, in the renewal of the liturgy. In a climate of prayer and under ecclesial supervision the whole Bible is presented to the people. Pertinent readings from both Testaments with a prayerful interlude from the Psalms are followed by a careful homily, opening the minds and the hearts of the people and inviting them to live God's revelation in their daily lives. The reaction of the disciples of Emmaus points out the ideal towards which all, priest and people, should strive: "Did not our hearts burn within us while he talked to us and explained the Scripture" (Lk 24:32)?

It is to be hoped that people will abandon the unfortunate casuistry by which they judged that they had not missed Mass provided they came in for the offertory. What they should understand is that, even if the law has not changed, to miss the liturgy of the word is a downright error of perspective and of Christian understanding of values.

The offertory rite has been abbreviated notably by the elimination of the Christmas prayer and of the epiclesis (invocation of the Holy Spirit) which anticipated the Eucharistic prayer. It is now simply the preparation of the oblates, a strict commentary of the words of institution: "The Lord took bread . . . wine." We do have the joy, however, of presenting our gifts in a formula which must be quite similar to the one originally used by our Lord at the Last Supper: "He took bread and blessed it." The gospel gives many examples of such blessings in which Jesus thanks his Father as he presents his request (Mt 11:25; Jn 11:41). The offertory blessing is also an invitation for us to bless God all day long as we go about our business, the work of our human hands, which we want to sanctify as we live in joyful thanksgiving.

The liturgy of the word places in our hands the revelation legacy of our Christian family, but it is the Eucharistic prayer which gives Scripture its maximal efficacy. Here the word becomes sacrament. The message of Christ becomes a personal presence. In the Eucharistic prayers renewal is at its best. A great benefit is to be found in the four Eucharistic prayers and all the new prefaces. We find here rich themes for meditation according to the rhythm of the liturgical cycle. Without abandoning its traditional patrimony (first canon) the Roman Church can find the expression of its piety in ancient formulas (second and third canons closely resembling the canon of Hippolytus) or in brand new creations (fourth canon) as the manifestation of a life which is always new yet always rooted in our Lord's Paschal mystery.

We more easily understand now the nature of the anaphora, the great Eucharistic prayer, and the relative importance of its different elements. Centering on the words of the Institution of the Eucharist, the heart and summit of all revelation, we affirm that Christ's saving event is at the same time history, presence, and anticipation (*anamnesis*); we invoke the Holy Spirit not only to transform the bread and wine, but ourselves also in Christ (*epiclesis*); we pray for the living and for the dead and finish with the solemn doxology, all of this vouched for by the great amen of the Congregation. Could a better school of prayer and meditation be imagined?

Christians formerly, gathered behind the priest who faced the orient, were keenly aware of the need of uniting their prayer to his in their approach to God. The new rites remind us graphically and forcibly that communion to Christ is also communion to his mystical body, and in practice union to our brothers in love. The rite of peace, the communion procession and song, underline this aspect without prejudice to the other which is favored by the times of silence recommended after communion and before the common prayers.

Ten

EUCHARISTIC RENEWAL

Today new positions, new emphases, manners of viewing are being developed about the Eucharist both on the level of theological thought and of pastoral action. These new orientations involve a restructuring of the Eucharistic mystery in its different aspects in order to achieve a total and synthetic grasp of Eucharistic doctrine in a fully dynamic way. This seems to be the preoccupation of the instruction of the Sacred Congregation of Rites on Eucharistic Worship, May 25, 1967.

The basic Vatican II text is probably that of the *Constitution on the Sacred Liturgy*, no. 47. "At the Last Supper, on the night when he was betrayed, our Savior instituted the Eucharistic Sacrifice of his body and blood. He did this in order to perpetuate the sacrifice of the Cross throughout the centuries until he should come again, and so to entrust to his beloved spouse, the Church, a memorial of his death and resurrection: a sacrament of love, a sign of unity, a bond of charity, a paschal banquet in which Christ is consumed, the mind is filled with grace and a pledge of future glory is given to us."

It appears that the fundamental reality of the Eucharist is its *memorial* character: memorial of our Lord's passion and resurrection by which is perpetuated the unique sacrifice of Calvary; memorial in which Christ gives himself as *food* under the signs of bread and wine making us participate in the benefits of the paschal sacrifice; a participation which makes actual the *new covenant* sealed once and for all by God with men, and which anticipates the eschatological banquet in the kingdom of our Father; a participation in joy and hope, in expectation (until he

comes), even impatience or at least prayer for the Lord's coming
(*maranatha*, Rv 22:20).

In fact, this memorial of the Lord extends to the whole work
of our salvation: to the past, the redemptive event; to the present,
the actual personal gift of Christ under the sign of food, realizing,
actualizing the event of our redemption; and to the future as
eschatological anticipation. Or better still, the Eucharistic memorial is seen in reference to the past and the future which meet
and blend in the present, a present of realization and of expectation, the present of the presence of the personal Christ, always
living and eternalized in his gift of himself.

Starting from the priesthood common to all Christians, the
Instruction *Eucharisticum Mysterium* insists on re-centering all
the aspects of the Eucharist around the Eucharistic celebration.
In the Eucharist we find a *unity of mystery* since sacrifice and
banquet belong to the same mystery (3b); unity of action since
the action is not only of Christ but also of all the Church (3c).
This unity finds its best expression in concelebration (47). There
is also unity of worship: the presence of Christ in the sacrament
derives from the sacrifice and tends, is ordained to sacramental
and spiritual communion (3e, g). And finally, existential unity:
starting from the Eucharist, man must strive to infuse, impregnate
the world with the spirit of Christ (50).

To this first, basic level of recentering the Eucharist in all its
constitutive elements around the community celebration of the
Eucharist as memorial, must be added an insistence on the revaluation of the Word of God in the Church, especially in the liturgical
celebration where word and sacrament should be understood together. "The preaching of the Word is needed for the very administration of the sacraments. For these are sacraments of faith,
and faith is born of the Word and nourished by it" (PO, no. 4).

This is so true, and the link between the liturgy of the Word
and the liturgy of the Eucharist is so close, that they "form one
single act of worship" (SC, no. 46): thus the word, or the liturgy
of the word, finds its integration and its plenitude, its fulfillment
in the sacrament of the Eucharistic liturgy. Such is the importance, the necessity of the word which enjoys a certain primacy.

The sacrament derives its power from a word which becomes fully efficacious when fully understood, enlisting the conscious, active, and fruitful participation of the faithful.

The sacrament is, as it were, a word efficacious and visible. It demands the context of the people of God in ecclesial assembly in order to receive always a little more of the salvation wrought in Christ. This profound unity of word-sacrament finds its most direct and perceptible expression in the Eucharist which is first of all a synaxis, a gathering together around the same altar, the place of sacrifice, under the direction of the bishop and his priests, to be united by communion at the Lord's table: the table of the word preparing the table of the bread (also in Jn, ch. 6).

It follows that the understanding of the different modes of the presence of Christ to his Church is necessary and fruitful, especially since it has assumed such importance in today's theological thought. Christ, in fact, is present, really present in the assembly of the faithful gathered in his name; in the Word, since it is he who speaks when the Scriptures are heard; in the person of the minister who offers the sacrifice, and above all under the species of the Eucharist (EM, no. 9).

Far from creating opposition, these different modes of Christ's presence lead to a better intelligence of the Eucharistic mystery, both in its celebration and in the salvific reality signified by the memorial and extending its influence to the whole of our Christian life.

How will this new approach affect our idea of the permanence of the presence of Christ under the Eucharistic species? Here again an evolution is taking place. Even in practice, the celebration of the Eucharist cannot be viewed as a means of perpetuating a presence, and this presence is no longer viewed in a static, independent way. Primacy belongs to the action, the time of the celebration. The presence of Christ under the sign of bread becomes by this sign, a sign-for-man; it finds its value outside of Mass, as an extension of the grace of the sacrifice. So considered, the real presence becomes the expression of a *dynamism of self-giving and communication*, and keeps us expecting the glorious final coming of Christ; for at each celebration of the memorial, we announce the death of the Lord until he comes. To be fully efficacious and meaningful the permanence of the presence of Christ under the Eucharistic species must be given this fully dynamic sense.

The celebration of the Eucharist and the life of the Church as the sacrament of the active presence of Christ are truly co-extensive and directed one to the other in mutual dependence.

It is no secret that Eucharistic devotions are experiencing a serious crisis; yet there is no reason why they cannot come out of it more authentic, true, and functional.

The hierarchy of values should not be problematic; the Mass is essential, devotions secondary.

In particular, the repetition of Masses of devotion is being questioned. Some priests, because of their need for functionality, authenticity, reality, might suffer from this rhythm of rapid succession, especially after experiencing normally a profound involvement of their religious consciousness in the first Mass.

Another problem is thanksgiving after Mass which is constantly recommended in all papal documents. The Instruction *Tres Abhinc annos* (no. 15) recommends a time of silent prayer before the Postcommunion. The profound purpose of this recommendation is clearly to integrate the interior, personal prayer of thanksgiving after Communion into the celebration of the Eucharist. In this manner, the Eucharistic devotion par excellence, a keen awareness and fostering by contemplative prayer of union with Christ, is absorbed into the celebration itself of the Mass.

The most acute problem today is perhaps the relation of *modern psychology* with Eucharistic devotions. As already pointed out the need is felt for authenticity, truth, useful purpose. Then the prevailing attitude of man at this moment in history can be called *personalist*. Abstract and schematized views of the world are important to him only if they relate to his existence and assist him in giving it depth and purpose.

There is also today a preference for inner city life, appreciation of community values, depreciation of separatist, especially isolating tendencies, disenchantment with accepted orthodoxies, accepted beliefs or practices, traditional or anti-traditional. This has been called the birth of the "third man" who desacralizes taboos, demythologizes fables, builds his own truth. Or in practical terms, the crisis of authority.

There is a continual extroversion, a propensity for finding one's satisfaction in external things or interest directed outward and favored by the pefection of the man, through the vast possibilities of social communication. A necessary conclusion is the consequent lack of esteem for any introversion, depreciation of the intellectual life of silence and recollection, prayer and meditation, examen of conscience, in one word of the interior, spiritual, ascetic life.

It is clear that traditional Eucharistic devotions are not favored by these modern psychological tendencies. In our secular world these devotions have a mythical and sacral, supposedly unreal, aspect that is judged quite unacceptable.

It would seem, therefore, that the only possibility of survival for these devotions lies in their integration with the Eucharistic celebration. The Mass, in fact, places the accent on the assembled congregation; it gives this community a dimension that surpasses human fraternity and finds its highest expression in the sacramental communion to the Body of Christ which supposes or demands complete personal commitment to the total Christ.

Eucharistic adoration and devotion will find its life and survival in the interior dimensions and the total requirements of Holy Communion and will thus come back to its origins, its fundamental structure (Jn 6:51).

This is the holy bread, the sacred banquet in which by receiving Christ we recall his death and glorious Resurrection and are filled with his grace, the pledge of our future glorification. And Christian grace seeks to communicate itself; love begins at home but cannot stay there.

I've got that joy deep in my heart and I want to share it all with God's children. Our Lord put it this way: "I have come to bring fire to the earth, and how I wish it were blazing already" (Lk 11:49). This is the fire lit on the Cross, a fire that should purify and inflame men's hearts, a fire that will draw all men to God with Christ and in Christ (Jn 12:32).

The recent Instructions from the Roman Congregations deserve special mention. The Instruction on "Sacramental Communion," issued by the Congregation for Divine Worship, June 29, 1970. The Instruction on "Facilitating Sacramental Communion in Particular Circumstances," issued by the Sacred Congregation for the Discipline of the Sacraments, Jan. 29, 1973. And the Instruction on "Holy Communion and Eucharistic Worship Outside the Mass," issued by the Congregation for Divine Worship, June 21, 1973.

Eleven

THEOLOGY OF THE NEW SACRAMENTARY

The new Sacramentary promulgated on Holy Thursday, March 26, 1970, has finally been translated and published in English. The use of this text became mandatory with the beginning of the new liturgical year on the first Sunday in Advent, December 1, 1974. The General Instruction of this Roman Missal gives an excellent summary of the actual Eucharistic faith of the post-Vatican II Church according to the old adage, "The Church's rule of prayer corresponds to the Church's enduring rule of faith" (2). Its introduction states clearly its purpose and spirit: it is meant as an adaptation to modern conditions (10-15), but as a witness to unchanging faith (2-5) and to unbroken tradition (6-9): faith in the sacrificial character of the Mass, faith in the real presence of Christ under the Eucharistic species, and faith in the unique role of the ministerial priest. These traditional Eucharistic emphases are in no way played down in our new missal. On the contrary they are given a better perspective within a wider framework of doctrine and practice. The new missal bears witness to the unity and coherence of the Church's tradition. It shows "the Church's concern for the Eucharist, its faith and its unchanging love of this great mystery" (1).

The Mass is a *sacrifice*. "The sacrifice of the Cross and its sacramental renewal in the Mass are, apart from the difference in the manner of offering, one and the same sacrifice" (2). "It is at once a sacrifice of praise and of thanksgiving, a sacrifice that reconciles us to the Father and makes amends to him for the sins of the world" (ibid). The Roman Canon (no. 1) is more explicit and emphatic about that. But the notions of memorial and of offering found in all the Canons bring home the same theology. For example, the third Eucharistic prayer states: "Look with favor on your Church's offering, and see the victim whose death has reconciled us to yourself." There is only one sacrifice, that of Christ, and no suggestion of repeating it, but a new emphasis on our participation in that sacrifice. We say, "we offer," "accept our offering" to express the consciousness of our identity with Christ through the Eucharist. The full paschal mystery is also put in clearer light; we are constantly reminded of Christ's "blessed passion, his resurrection from the dead and his glorious ascension," especially by the acclamations after the words of institution. In the person of our risen Lord, whose supper we share, we are caught up into the redemptive process at its very source, as we plunge into it sacramentally again and again, until we are admitted to the banquet of eternity of which the Eucharist is the pledge and foretaste.

The Instruction emphasizes the special *real presence* of Christ in the consecrated bread and wine but without prejudice to his other real presences in the whole sacramental action. "The Church believes that the Lord Jesus is really present among us in a wonderful way in the Eucharistic species. The second Vatican Council and the other pronouncements of the Church's magisterium have reaffirmed the same doctrine and the same meaning proposed by the Council of Trent for our belief. At Mass this presence of Christ is proclaimed not only by the words of consecration by which Christ is made present through transubstantiation, but also by the sense of deep reverence and adoration which are evident in the liturgy of the Eucharist. His presence is further recognized by Christians when they honor the Eucharist in a special way on Holy Thursday and on Corpus Christi" (3). Eucharistic devotion is thus shown as solidly grounded in the liturgy and leading back to it, according to the directives of the Constitution on the Sacred Liturgy (no. 13).

Christ is also present in other ways in the sacred liturgy, by means of which his loving concern and saving action reach us. "The Lord's Supper or Mass gathers together the people of God, with a priest presiding in the person of Christ, to celebrate the memorial of the Lord or Eucharistic sacrifice. For this reason the promise of Christ is particularly true of such a local congregation of the Church: 'Where two or three are gathered in my name, there am I in their midst' (Mt 18:20). In the celebration of Mass, which perpetuates the sacrifice of the cross, Christ is really present in the assembly itself, which is gathered in his name, in the person of the minister, in his word, and indeed substantially and unceasingly under the Eucharistic species" (7). "Within the community of the faithful a priest possesses the power of orders to offer sacrifice in the person of Christ. At the Eucharist by his actions and by his proclamations of the word he should impress upon the faithful the living presence of Christ" (60).

About Christ's presence in his word, the Instruction states: "When the scriptures are read in the Church, God himself speaks to his people, and it is Christ, present in the word who proclaims the Gospel (9).

The special presence of Christ in the sacrament is indicated by the words of consecration; by the preceding prayer in which we ask that through God's blessing and the power of the Holy Spirit the bread and wine may become for us the body and blood of Christ; by the way the bread and cup are subsequently spoken of as life-giving, saving; and by the way they are handled, reverenced, and received (56g, 233, 247g).

The immediate finality of the real presence is holy Communion which is the only full participation in the Mass. The Eucharist is for us the bread of life and our spiritual drink: "Take and eat . . . Take and drink." The grace it offers is the peace and unity of the kingdom. But it is simply not true that adoration of Christ is something secondary in the Eucharist. On the contrary, the basis, the foundation of the whole rite is the recognition of Christ for what he is, namely, our risen Lord. Christ is present as our sacrificial food and operates by drawing us with him in his ascent to his Father, into the movement of his life, death, and resurrection.

A special new feature of the new order of the Mass is found in the times of social silence. These are clearly times of personal, private prayer which evidently has its place even in communal worship. The Instruction specifies: "Silence should be observed at designated times as part of the celebration. Its character will depend on the time it occurs in the particular celebration. At the penitential rite and again after the invitation to pray, each one should become recollected; at the conclusion of a reading or the homily, each one meditates briefly on what he has heard; after communion, he praises God in his heart and prays" (23). The foreword to our English edition adds: "In order to facilitate the use of silence rubrical directions for silent prayer have been indicated in this edition. These silent periods should not be too brief or too lengthy. A more lengthy pause may take place at the penitential rite and after the readings or homily. The proper use of periods of silent prayer and reflection will help to render the celebration less mechanical and impersonal and lend a more prayerful spirit to the liturgical rite. Just as there should be no celebration without song, so too there should be no celebration without periods for silent prayer and reflection" (p. 13*). The Instruction itself has a special note relative to the Canon of the Mass: "All should listen to the Eucharistic prayer in silent reverence and share in it by making the acclamation" (55). In the Directory for Masses with Children we find: "Even in Masses with children silence should be observed at the proper time as a part of the celebration, lest too great a role be given to external action. In their own way children are genuinely capable of reflection. They need, however, a kind of introduction so that they will learn how to reflect within themselves, meditate briefly, or praise God and pray to him in their hearts, for example, after the homily or after communion" (p. 57*).

The Instruction's theology of the Canon of the Mass is also noteworthy (54-55). "The Eucharistic prayer, a prayer of thanksgiving and sanctification, is the center and high point of the entire celebration. The meaning of the prayer is that the whole congregation joins Christ in acknowledging the works of God and in offering the sacrifice." The chief elements of the Eucharistic prayer are enumerated and explained briefly. They are thanksgiving, acclamation, epiclesis, the narrative of the institution and the consecration, *anamnesis* (memorial of Christ's passion, death, and resurrection), offering, intercessions, and final doxology. The epiclesis is the invocation that by God's power and Spirit the gifts may become the body and blood of Christ, and that we may become one body, one Spirit in Christ.

The Instruction distinguishes clearly between the ministerial priesthood, the sacrament of Holy Orders, and the general priesthood of all believers because of their baptism (4-5). The ministerial priest has a unique role. "He offers sacrifice in the person of Christ and presides over the assembly of God's holy people" (4). The new rite highlights his presidented role and his ministry of word and sacrament, the heart of his pastoral responsibilities. But the new rite also underlines the ecclesial nature of the Eucharist by promoting the active participation of the people and insisting that "the celebration of the Eucharist is the action of the whole Church." "Greater attention is given to some aspects of the Eucharistic celebration which have sometimes been overlooked in the course of time. The worshipping community is the people of God, won by Christ with his blood, called together by the Lord, nourished by his blood. It is a people called to offer God the prayers of the entire human family, a people which gives thanks in Christ for the mystery of salvation by offering his sacrifice. It is a people brought together and strengthened in unity by sharing in the body and blood of Christ. This people is holy in origin, but by conscious, active, and fruitful participation in the mystery of the Eucharist it constantly grows in holiness" (5). The ordained priest does not stand outside the community but within it. The unique and essential role of the priest is given the context which clarifies its proper understanding. By their active participation the people's faith is brought into play and strengthened. In particular, within the Eucharistic prayer they proclaim the mystery of faith, say Amen to what is said and done especially at the all important moment of communion.

Of interest also are other theological statements of the Instruction. On the purpose or ends of the sacrifice of the Mass: "It is at once a sacrifice that reconciles us to the Father and makes amends to him for the sins of the world" (2). On the general structure of the Mass: "Although the Mass is made up of the liturgy of the word and the liturgy of the Eucharist, the two parts are so closely connected as to form one act of worship. The table of God's word and of Christ's body is prepared and from it the faithful are instructed and nourished" (8). On the liturgy of the Eucharist: "Christ took bread and the cup, gave thanks and gave to his disciples saying, 'Take and eat, this is my body. Take and drink, this is the cup of my blood. Do this in memory of me.' The Church has arranged the celebration of the Eucharistic liturgy to correspond to these words and actions of Christ. In the preparation of the gifts, bread, wine, and water are brought to the altar, the same elements which Christ used. The Eucharistic prayer is the hymn of thanksgiving to God for the whole work of salvation; the offerings become the body and blood of Christ. The breaking of the one bread is a sign of the unity of the faithful, and in communion they receive the body and blood of Christ as the Apostles did from his hands" (48).

On concelebration: "This is done not to add external solemnity but to express in a clearer light the mystery of the Church, which is the sacrament of unity" (59). "In a special way concelebration shows the unity of priesthood and of the sacrifice, and the unity of the people of God" (153). On reservation of the Eucharist: "It is highly recommended that the holy Eucharist be reserved in a chapel suitable for private adoration and prayer" (276). Finally, some might be surprised to find the detailed directions for Communion under both species from a tube (248-250) and from a spoon (251-252).

Twelve

EUCHARISTIC SPIRITUALITY TODAY

If theology is the knowledge of God and of the supernatural, and if spirituality is spiritual-mindedness, an ingrained outlook on God that guides and colors our actions, theology and spirituality are clearly closely related. Eucharistic spirituality would then be the mind of Christ ("Do this in memory of me," 1 Cor 11:24) and the logic of the Spirit ("It is the Spirit that gives life," Jn 6:63) as directing and inspiring our reactions to the Eucharistic mystery.

To put it briefly, today the great patristic insights into the meaning of the Eucharist, themselves extrapolated from scripture and experience under the Spirit, are again coming into their own. The Eucharistic presence, of course, is valued as the objective presence of the risen Lord, but the Eucharist is more clearly seen as the kingdom of God in action, the manifesto, not only in word but also in deed, of all that Christ has done, is doing, and will do to change the world, by living in the people of God and using them for his own purposes, serving notice of the new order upon the world.

This new but always ancient spirituality is based on the recovered understanding of the patristic notion of offering and self-offering; of thanksgiving for creation and the world as well as for the re-creation in Christ and his Spirit; of the recapitulation of all things in Christ, the remembering and re-presentation of his death, resurrection, and ascension into heaven, and of his gift of his Spirit at Pentecost, so that they all become active and potent in the present to constitute the people of God; of the sense of receiving the mystery of each other as well as of ourselves in the Eucharistic elements, since together we are Christ's body (1 Cor 12:27) and as parts of it we belong to each other (Rm 12:5); the sense of penetrating into the mystery of God in Christ by doing and experiencing all this, by feeding on the very fruits of the remembered and pleaded (Rm 8:34) sacrifice; the sense of God's love, "that liquor sweet and most divine, which my God feels as blood, but I as wine."

The understanding of the essence of Christian spirituality today centers on the relationship between the love of God and the love of neighbor. Many people experience difficulty in relating these two loves, their devotional life and their life of service to their family and to society at large. Some have sometimes been tempted to consider time spent in prayerful contemplation of God and his revealed mysteries as time stolen from involvement with one's fellow man, especially when he is suffering great physical oppression from disease, racial injustice, or economic starvation. This view often leads to effective social action, but frequently to the exclusion of any direct relationship between Christians and God at all. Love of neighbor, thus isolated from love of God, becomes an excuse for repairing the secular universe on its own terms, re-establishing the kingdom of this world, so to speak, while God and religion become unnecessarily pious afterthoughts.

The love of God cannot be realized only in love of our neighbor. That is not the meaning of the Gospel saying, "In so far as you did this to one of the least of these brothers of mine, you did it to me" (Mt 25:40). Our love of our neighbor is something which has its source in a prior act of God as he loves us and as we respond to that love. Love for men is characteristic of the Father (1 Jn 4:8, 16) and he proves this love by delivering up his Son (1 Jn 3:16-18). Whoever lives in union with God must live a life of light, virtue, and love, and keep God's commandments, especially the commandment to love all human beings (1 Jn 2:10-11, 3:10).

The same problem of the two loves that we find in the general discussion of present-day spirituality appears also in our Eucharistic practice. We might portray this tension within present-day Eucharistic spirituality as one between the supernaturalist and the naturalist position, between transcendentalist and secularist views.

There is the tendency among what may itself be a legitimate diversity of practice to stress either the God-ward side of the Eucharist or its man-ward side.

The Eucharist is an act whereby we join Christ as he makes the perfect offering of praise, thanksgiving, propitiation, and supplication to God, for and on behalf of all mankind. It is the link between heaven and earth where in Christ the community of the Church is joined to God and through the Church mankind is brought into communion with him. Now one may be attracted by the specialized religious acts of worship, precisely because they speak of the transcendent, the non-secular, of God's gracious act of loving which is the source of all our loving. One could also at the same time neglect to relate his religious life to the ethical action which has to be carried out in a society whose patterns and norms of behavior are increasingly secular. On the contrary, one could concentrate his attention much more closely on the love of the brotherhood, but at the cost of losing sight of God's act of originating love, with the consequent danger that the idea of fellowship becomes less than Christian, a mere human getting-together, rather than a fellowship in Christ. An extreme case would be found where the Eucharist would no longer be seen as the *source* of Christian love but as a ritual-expression of the love which is already present and being exercised within the community, the service of the community being seen primarily, if not exclusively in its ethical and social context. There is no reason, however, why both views, the supernaturalist and the naturalist could not go hand in hand, as we see them operative, for example, in the renewed emphasis on devotion to the reserved sacrament among the followers of Charles de Foucauld, the Little Brothers and Sisters of Jesus, and the religious of Mother Teresa's Congregation. The rule of life of these modern apostles of the poor and destitute asks these religious to pray at least one hour each day before the blessed Sacrament.

Opposition to the transcendentalist view of the Eucharist is voiced on several scores and not completely without reason. The ritual acts of worship are often too sharply distinguished from the community's social acts. The usual Eucharistic congregation, the community at Sunday Mass practically everywhere, we are told, lacks the personal touch of real friendship and is at best remotely friendly and mostly anonymous. This objection, however, is based on a vaguely romantic idea of friendship and community. There is a whole psychology of the nature and friendliness of gatherings involving great multitudes, for example, at political rallies or athletic events. Hardly anyone who has attended a solemn liturgy in one of the world's great basilicas, or even a religious rally, can fail to be impressed by the unity and catholicity of Christ's Church.

There is also the question of symbols and their subjection to change according to the people, the society that uses them: shepherds naturally will speak of lambs, monarchists of kings, banana, potato, or peanut growers of their own respective products. This question of symbols deserves our special attention. Briefly, the thesis is this. The only way we can speak of the mystery of God is by way of analogy and in human terminology. Now, even the official Biblical revelation needs to be demythologized, to be relieved of the elements that are characteristic of particular conditions, economic, social, and political. This is the only way that the core, the essential revelation can be reached and assimilated, while avoiding a distorted view not only of God but also of the universe.

The concrete exemplification of symbols is of central importance within a given society. Those symbols which are closely related to the particular livelihood of a particular cultic and political structure are much more likely to be superseded and become obsolete, for example, symbols like lambs, crowns, thrones, scepters, and even altars for people who have never witnessed a bloody sacrifice.

All symbols, or even etiological facts (facts that need to be interpreted, like birth and death) are more or less relative and need interpretation, since they may be regarded differently within different societies. Some symbols, however, are less relative than others because they are connected to basic goods and requirements, like bread, water, light, life, breath, fire, wine. In the Eucharist the use of bread and wine appeals to a universal age-old, world-wide experience: that of hunger and thirst. Bread and wine are symbolic of food in its most nourishing form, and wine is for banquets and special occasions. The Eucharistic worship, however, although it is conceived as an act of communion between the believer and God, has also an essential relation to the death and resurrection of Jesus of Nazareth. This is where further explanation will be required based on the words of Jesus himself (Jn 6:51-58) and the understanding of the primitive Church (1 Cor 11:24-32). The total Eucharistic mystery will then appear as the food of our spiritual life, a memorial of all the works of God, a proclamation of the death of our Lord, a sign of his perpetual presence among his own, the communion of his body and blood, the renewing of our covenant with God, a sharing of the Spirit, the remission of our sins, the healing of our soul's sicknesses, and the rest of our conscience. The transcendentalist view of the Eucharist might too easily stop here, glossing over the fact that Christian worship is also the meeting of God's people, a call to brotherly love, the proclamation of Christ's new commandment, the redemption of the sins of the world and the salvation of its multitudes, the building up of the body of Christ in the fervor of the Spirit of Christian love.

Christian worship is essentially Eucharistic worship, and worship is an essential part of Christian spirituality. We simply cannot substitute theology or even private personal devotion for worship. Yet Christian spirituality has always stressed the element of personal choice and decision. And personal prayer is a necessary and perhaps even primary aspect of corporate acts of Christian worship. Nothing can replace mental and personal prayer which is the soul of all prayer, private or communal. This being the case it is a bit surprising to see that acts of private, personal, Eucharistic devotion which should be the normal extension of the grace of the Eucharistic celebration and a remote preparation for the next celebration, that these forms of private devotion (silent prayer before and after the service, mental prayer before the Blessed Sacrament, Eucharistic benedictions) have recently been largely discarded in the name of the corporate nature of the Eucharist. There is no doubt that such devotions give unmistakable expression to a transcendentalist view of Christian worship, but it is no less true that no one really can love his neighbor if he does not love God, and that prayer is still the soul of all apostolates.

It is also true, however, that the transcendentalist view of the Eucharist as the Lamb's high feast in which the dominant symbols are those of priesthood and kingship, should not make one lose sight of Jesus' last meal with his faltering disciples before going into the garden on his way to the cross. The great merit of the symbolism of kingship is that it speaks of the transcendency of God, as Lord of all creation, and brings home the fact that our religious acts are directed to the Lord and source of all reality and are in no sense private, special acts. Yet it is also a fact that, "All that showy pomp of splendor, all that sheen of angel wings, Was but borrowed from the baubles that surround our earthly kings." When symbols are divorced from the existing social realities they may have a positively deleterious effect in their religious use. God is not a tyrannical, pathological king, nor is he a "Big-Daddy-up-aloft."

In actual Eucharistic theology the images of sacrifice, kingship and the like, are being played down in the actions of the celebrant and his position at the altar; a greater stress has been laid on the corporate nature of the meal, the sharing of the one Bread, on those symbols which are less relative, and that is wise. Yet it should be evident also that there is only one essential revelation from God in Christ and that it is complete and unrepeatable. There can never be any question, for example, of instituting new sacraments or of discarding any of those that are found in our Christian tradition. Time should quicken rather than destroy, yet there is no reason why venerable ancient tradition should be allowed to be crusted over with a leprosy of routine.

Thirteen

THE SACRED AND THE SECULAR

The profound changes now apparent in man's reaction to religion stem from different mentalities, different interpretations of human experience, or rather different emphases given to human anthropology, to the conception of man and his relations to God and the universe in which we live. There is also the question of authenticity which our contemporaries, especially younger people, regard as a fundamental requirement of human existence. Authentic existence is achieved by personal decision and involvement, complete sincerity and honesty, as opposed to sham, pretense, hypocrisy; words or actions cannot be without interior meaning or purpose.

There is a secularized mentality which stresses man's autonomy, his efforts to achieve self-awareness in immediate experience. For all practical purposes man seems to live without God. He controls his environment, and the whole of reality is the object of his knowledge and constant research. Know-how, not prayer, takes him to the moon. This secular conception of man stresses his autonomy, his initiative, his responsibility, his commitment to a better future. Man's relation to God is rejected by many secular-minded people as a stupefying illusion; others acknowledging man's relation to God as a supreme value, conceive earthly development as a collaboration with him but seek union with God especially in the union of all men.

Another very different conception of man has prevailed for a long time, a sacralized conception which is based on another kind of experience, and stresses God's initiative in man's life, a revelation made known to us through a mediator, Jesus Christ.

It acknowledges God at the summit of all earthly forces, and dependence on God as the divine Absolute. God's greatest gift to man is freedom which, however, should be exercised as a response to the divine will. God remains essentially inaccessible but gave man sacred institutions, especially as remedy for sin, but ultimately in view of union with his creature by sharing with him his divine nature (2 P 1:4).

These two views of man, the sacred and the secular, have their own merits and weaknesses, and may validly be accentuated according to circumstances, but should really be co-ordinated since they are mutually complementary. Human autonomy is perhaps sometimes minimized in the sacralized outlook; conversely, God cannot be left out of man's life or be considered merely in a one-sided relationship in which he exists merely to serve man. For man is called not only to seek the protection of the divine force, but to love God for his own sake, even to share the divine nature.

There are very practical consequences which follow from the sacred and secular mentalities. For example, Christians have sometimes been tempted to consider time spent in prayerful contemplation of God and his revealed mysteries as time stolen from involvement with one's fellow man, especially when one's fellow man is suffering great physical oppression from disease, racial injustice, or economic starvation. This view often leads to effective social action, but frequently to the exclusion of any direct relationship between Christians and God at all. Love of neighbor, thus isolated from love of God, becomes an excuse for repairing the secular universe on its own terms, re-establishing the kingdom of this world, so to speak, while neglecting the kingdom of God, God and religion becoming unnecessary pious after-thoughts.

Vatican II offers a balanced position of the problem. "It is of the essence of the Church that she be both human and divine, visible yet invisibly endowed, eager to act yet devoted to contemplation, present in this world and yet not at home in it. She is all these things in such a way that in her the human is directed and subordinated to the divine, the visible likewise to the invisible, action to contemplation, and this present world to that city yet to come, which we seek" (SC, no. 2).

In particular, the contemporary theology of the Eucharist has been re-interpreted in a more secularized sense, but this should be done in complete fidelity with the essential elements of the Eucharistic mystery.

Liturgists today stress the union which should exist between life and liturgy, rejecting anything which would make the Eucharist a celebration devoid of all contact with life, while encouraging encounter between the participants and anything which will strengthen the relationship between prayer and the daily joys and needs of men. Yet the Eucharist is much more than a family celebration or a gathering of friends. Liturgical celebrations and the actions of our daily life are interrelated, since all our actions can and should be directed to God in union with Christ (Col 3:17; 1 Cor 10:31), but they are in no sense interchangeable. It may be impossible to situate exactly the moment when a boy becomes a man yet the two are essentially different. Likewise it is false to claim that an act of beneficence is as Eucharistic, if not more so, than the private week-day Mass or a devout priest. The sacramental action differs in kind from an ordinary daily action through the mode of divine intervention in each case, and life has different dimensions, different relations to the world, to God, to eschatology, each of which has its own value and should be respected.

A sacralized outlook may throw out of focus a quest of God for his own sake or the lovable nature of man because of God's love for him, while a secularized mentality may over-emphasize man's natural need of being loved for what he is. A balanced Eucharistic approach will use the mutual encounter of the sacrament as a means of meeting the Lord and one's neighbor in the Lord. The goal of mutual assistance must be our common acknowledgment of Christ as the source of Christian unity. It is not the Christians who make Christ Eucharistically present through their efforts to unite, but Christ himself who comes to us in order to unite us more closely to him and to one another. Yet every act of beneficence is a step in the right direction, and a purely natural act of human love in no way excludes a love of

God which is not explicitly included.

In relation to eschatology, the secularized mentality will celebrate the Eucharist as a prayer for a better future on earth, as a commitment of all participants to work for the advent of a better world, an earthly, temporal, constantly progressing world. The Paschal victory over death will be given an earthly meaning of a gradual victory over certain sociological structures which oppress man, and over anything which prevents him from living at peace with himself or with his fellow men. There is no reason, however, why this short-range view of the progress of charity on earth could not go hand-in-hand with the expectation of God's more perfect promise and gift of a definitive love beyond the grave.

The Paschal mystery itself will be differently emphasized according to the two mentalities being considered. The sacralizing mentality will emphasize God's initiative and refer to the Passover in terms of God's intervention to liberate man and establish a new covenant with him, in Jesus Christ. The Eucharist will then be the celebration of our faithfulness to God and of God's faithfulness to us. On the other hand, a catechesis which emphasizes man's effort will refer to the Passover and its celebration in the Eucharist in terms of life's victory over death and the triumph of meaning over meaninglessness, a victory which constitutes man's liberation in the world.

The richness of the Paschal mystery evidently calls for a variety of catechetical approaches which complement each other and respect the essential while differing in their accentuations. If union with God in Jesus Christ is stressed, it should be clearly indicated how our union with God invites us to achieve a more perfect union with all men, and how it gives us the strength to do so. On the other hand, it is essential to point out that Christ's resurrection transcends the progress of a renewed earthly life. The Eucharistic celebration is the active memorial which Jesus instituted so that we may share in his Paschal event. This means sharing not only in its fruits, enlightenment, encouragement, forgiveness of our sins, but also in the very act whereby he gives himself to the Father. Finally, the Eucharistic celebration will acquire its true meaning only if it includes the relationship to the specifically Christian reality which Jesus came to reveal and fulfill: namely, our union with God in him, the Son of God made man and now reigning in glory. For it is, in fact, this union which leads us to fullness of life and is the constant source of an increasingly profound and universal love for all men.

A powerful conviction permeates the New Testament that before all else, the primary manner of Christ's existence now is as the Lord Jesus in the glory of his transfigured humanity, the first-born of creation, the first-fruits of the resurrection. The radical meaning of all life, of all liturgy is this celebration of Christ's existence as Lord, embracing an ascending worship and a descending sanctification. It is the Lord present at the right hand of the Father, and therefore transcending the sacramental order who thus offers to his Church, in the Eucharistic signs, the special gift of himself. The Lord who thus comes to his people in the power of the Holy Spirit is the Lord of glory. Only within this primary mode of Christ's existence does it make any sense to talk of Christ present in the ways we try to list: his abiding presence with the Church, in the assembled community at prayer, in our hearts, in God's word of salvation or judgment, in the very Eucharist itself. This New Testament conviction of Christ's presence is not so tidily nor diminishingly pigeon-holed in a scale of priorities governed by intricacy rather than by depth.

Especially in relation to the Eucharistic sacrifice the secularized mentality needs more correctives. It does not like the word sacrifice precisely because of its sacral connotation. Worship must be especially a love in action practicing obedience, justice, and charity in relation to our neighbor. This is our gift to God, an existential sacrifice, and the meal men share provides a very natural symbol. In this outlook the priest is not really a ritual-mediator but the one who animates the faithful and refers to God the union of the community.

This approach has the great advantage of focusing attention on the union which should exist between the participants in the Eucharistic celebration and the social commitment of true Christian love. But it also minimizes the community's orientation towards God by its emphasized orientation towards men. Prayer to God is practically replaced by the participants' exchange of ideas or communication of sentiments. The Old Testament (Am 5:21-22) already indicates God's abhorrence for empty ritual sacrifices which would not express an obedience and justice lived in our ordinary actions. But the liturgy loses its specific character if the Eucharistic gathering no longer differs sufficiently and clearly from an ordinary meal or an encounter on the human level. And Christ's priestly role, especially his eternal priesthood, cannot be overlooked. A valid interpretation of the Eucharist must make explicit reference to Christ's sacrifice and to the function of the priest as Christ's representative. The Eucharist is Jesus personally present under a double form, in his consecration to the Father accomplished so that we too may be united to the Father (Jn 17:19) precisely by sharing in his act of self-giving. Before being a meal shared between men, the Eucharist is truly a meal in which God invites us to his table. All of us are invited to the same table and are expected to come with the disposition of our Lord himself: "In your minds you must be the same as Christ Jesus" (Ph 2:5). And so our union with God gives greater perfection to our mutual union, which should be communion in Jesus Christ, and from celebration to celebration become progressively more perfect.

The Eucharist is essentially a reference to Christ in the Paschal act of his death and resurrection, and the participation of all Christians in this mystery. An authentic Eucharist must therefore include the desire for union with God, the effort to realize union between all men, and the hope which transcends death, all of this through Christ, with him, and in him.

Fourteen

EUCHARISTIC LIVING

A priest, after the example of Christ, must be a good shepherd, ready to give even his life for his sheep (Jn 10:11), but he must also live in close union with the Father in the Holy Spirit. "I know the Father and I lay down my life for my sheep" (14). Without the experience of God which matures into love, the priest will be a mere hireling who has no real concern for the sheep (13).Union with God, which is the nature and object of Christian prayer, springs from our faith and is manifested in our love for our neighbor (1 Jn 1:3).

Vatican II (PO, no. 18), dealing with the priest's spiritual life, sees the danger of scattering our energy in all directions in our effort to meet the vexing problems of our day. To remedy this situation, Christ must be our life's fulcrum and the Eucharist the tap-root, the source of the pastoral love which is the bond of priestly perfection. "But this goal cannot be achieved unless priests themselves penetrate ever more deeply through prayer into the mystery of Christ."

The external works of the ministry or even personal devotional practices will not of themselves unify our life. "Priests attain to the unity of their lives by uniting themselves with Christ in acknowledging the Father's will and in the gift of themselves on behalf of the flock committed to them." Without this personal union with Christ there cannot be an active and fruitful participation in the Eucharist, the source and root of pastoral love and of the apostolic activity of the Church.

A Christian must live the Paschal mystery, the mystery of the death and resurrection of Christ, which is represented and reproduced in the Eucharistic celebration. But to draw effectively from this source of life there are certain necessary dispositions which are cultivated by praying to the Father not only in secret (Mt 6:6) but even constantly (1 Th 5:17). The Eucharist which is the summit of the Christian life must be prolonged, incarnated and expressed in the ordinary duties of everyday life, in the works of pastoral love, in personal devotion as well as in apostolic work; but this is impossible without personal prayer.

The priest will unify his interior and exterior life, his contemplation and his action, by union with Christ, the principle and source of his life. His personal holiness should flow from his ministry, exercised in faith and motivated by the love which the Holy Spirit pours in open hearts (Rm 5:5). That is why the Council urges: "that they may discharge their ministry with fidelity, they should prize daily conversation with Christ the Lord in visits of personal devotion to the most Holy Eucharist" (PO, no. 18). Some may be disaffected by the structure, formalized nature of this statement, but the principle of personal, mental, private Eucharistic prayer is what is really important and essentially meant.

It would be a grave error to imagine that a priest's interior life consists uniquely or in greater part in exercises of piety or even in personal prayer, and that it is only by them that the priest attains union with Christ in the exercise of his ministry, and so unifies his life. Such an approach is false as the Council has pointed out. The priest's holiness flows from his ministry and all the duties of his state in life (PO, no. 8). Prayer alone would not suffice since he must learn to live according to the Gospel, put in practice the charity of Christ, grow constantly in faith, hope and charity, and so develop his spirit of prayer (OT, no. 8).

The dichotomy between prayer and apostolic action is probably the reason why in practice personal prayer today, if it is not rejected theoretically, is actually at a low ebb. The result is a relaxation of serious interior, spiritual living with all its consequences. In such an atmosphere, even in seminaries, silence and recollection have little or no meaning and a complete breakdown occurs in the observance of external rules and regulations. Even the Eucharistic celebration, in spite of all the liturgical renewal, does not produce all the expected fruits, and initial fervor dies in discouragement or simple inanition.

This sad situation is probably due to the fact that personal prayer has not been solidly grounded in the liturgy and in the Eucharist. It has not been sufficiently directed to and derived from the Eucharistic celebration. It has lacked the strength and freshness of the word of God which is the marrow of the liturgy. The remedy is immediately available. Personal prayer must derive from the liturgy and prepare for it. There is a necessary mutual relation between personal prayer and the Eucharistic celebration. Moreover, any apostolic activity which does not emanate from the altar and find there its full measure of success appears suspect. Any exercise of piety or personal devotion which develops without reference to the Eucharist, or in opposition to the liturgy, is doomed to sterility and death.

The Eucharist, the memorial of the passion of our Lord, the joyful banquet in which one eats and drinks the body and blood of Christ, the anticipation of the coming heavenly kingdom, this wonderful sacrament should be the food in which Christian and priestly prayer finds its nourishment. The mystery of the death and resurrection of Christ, represented and reproduced in the Eucharistic celebration in which he participates actively, will give the priest's life its true dimension which is that of the Cross of Christ. The joy and satisfaction of sitting at the banquet of the Lamb will help us to discover that love is always the pure source of the truest joy. The Eucharist will also plant in the priest an eschatological tension, an efficacious desire of establishing the true kingdom of God on earth, by changing it as much as possible to some kind of anticipated heaven in which God is all in all.

Personal prayer, however, must not be confused with forms or methods of prayer which are so unpopular with people today, especially the younger generation, with their often boorish approach, their self-satisfaction and general discontent with others, their apparent insensitiveness to others' feelings or unwillingness to make themselves agreeable. Yet the Council referring to the different means of support for a priestly life notes that there are some common and particular means, but also some new ones which the Spirit of God never ceases to stir up in the people of God and which the Church commends for the sanctification of all her members (PO, no. 18).

Thus a sensitivity session may run the risk of degenerating into a systematic destructive criticism of everybody and everything. Yet it could also be the occasion for a transformation of one's life in the light of serious criticism and lead to a more fruitful participation in the Paschal mystery by extending its influence in our everyday life.

Silence in particular is not in high favor today, even if recent Church documents on the liturgy and the Eucharist have underlined in theory and in practice the spiritual value and necessity of prayerful silence: witness the moments of silence and recollection prescribed in the new order of the Mass. The great mistress of the spiritual life, the saintly doctor Theresa of Avila, defined personal prayer as "dealing with friendly matters, speaking often with God whom we know loves us." Silence, interior and exterior silence, is the necessary and indispensable atmosphere for prayer, not only to enter into dialog with God, but also to find full profit and satisfaction in heavenly things.

Pope Paul VI in his encyclical *Mysterium Fidei* (nos. 67-70) underlines the benefits of intimate colloquies with our Lord in the Blessed Sacrament both for our personal and social life. Christ as our Emmanuel dwells with us, full of grace and truth. He restores morality, nourishes virtues, consoles the afflicted, strengthens the weak. He proposes his own example to those who come to him that all may learn to be, like himself, meek and humble of heart and to seek not their own interests but those of God. "Anyone who approaches this august sacrament with special devotion and endeavors to return generous love for Christ's own infinite love will experience and fully understand how precious is the life hidden with Christ in God (Col 3:3) and how great is the value of converse with Christ, for there is nothing more consoling on earth, nothing more efficacious for advancing along the road of holiness." He will cultivate a social love by which the common good is given preference over the good of the individual, and an active ecclesial spirit which makes its own the cause of the Church, especially its peace and unity.

It should be clear, however, that the essential worship of the Eucharist is the celebration of the Mass which draws us into an ever deeper participation in the Paschal mystery by spiritual communion with Christ. Eucharistic prayer outside the Mass is recommended provided it "harmonizes with the liturgy, is in some way derived from it and leads people toward the liturgy as to something which of its nature is far superior to these devotions" (SC, no. 13). That is the meaning of the exhortation found in the Instruction on Eucharistic worship (no. 50): "The faithful should strive to worship our Lord in the Blessed Sacrament, in harmony with their way of life. Pastors should exhort them to this and set them a good example."

The coordination of the Eucharistic celebration with private personal prayer is a delicate problem especially in our seminaries and religious houses of formation. The keynote of a solution seems to be flexibility as opposed to ironclad rigidity. One should also bear in mind that the celebration of the Eucharist is of its nature communitarian, whereas personal prayer takes place in the depth of our soul. Yet the Mass must include personal private prayer, and group meditative prayer is surely beneficial.

Both the celebration of the Eucharist and personal mental prayer clearly have their respective places, for example, in the life of the seminary community. It does not follow, however, that their practice should be controlled by obligatory disciplinary regulations. The trend today is toward personal responsibility, an approach that is completely spontaneous and free. This atmosphere of sincerity and confidence is clearly recommended by the Council (OT, no. 11). Yet a seminarian (or a religious) who could not be led to desire and live the Eucharistic celebration as a high point in his life, and would not appreciate personal mental prayer as a joyful intimate encounter with God, preparing for and extending into his life the grace of the Mass, would not be apt for the priesthood (or the religious life).

Fifteen

THE EUCHARIST AND THE CHURCH

The most characteristic action of the Church has always been the celebration of the Eucharist. From its earliest days the Church has always found around the altar its fullest life and the truest manifestation of its intimate nature.

The Church and the Eucharist are so intimately related that in God's actual plan for our salvation, one cannot exist or survive without the other. In fact, the Church celebrates and effects the Eucharist, yet it is especially the Eucharist, sacrament and sacrifice, which makes the Church what it is essentially, the mystical body of Christ, a community of believers and worshippers.

The Church can be considered as a visible, historical society founded by Christ and given the power to sanctify men. But the Church is also and especially the perennial event of salvation being worked out in God's people. Through the celebration of the Eucharist these two complementary aspects of the Church, the body of Christ, are given full dimension.

The visible, social, organizational character of the Church has sometimes overshadowed, if not actually obstructed, the interior, spiritual life which the Church should promote and manifest to the world. The Church's institutional, hierarchical character constantly tends to attract all the attention. Theologians enumerating the qualities or characteristics of the Church state that the Church is visible, indestructible, infallible, one, holy, Catholic, and apostolic. The holiness of the Church seems lost in the forest of the historical institution. Without depreciating this horizontal dimension of the Church growing and developing its essential structures in the course of time and history, more attention should be paid to the vertical, heavenward dimension.

The Church, in fact, is mysteriously identified with her risen and glorious savior. It is his mystical body, making continuously and efficaciously available the event of our salvation. The Church is not merely a place for meeting or even a society of believers. It is above all a builder of community, of common sharing in the saving events wrought by Christ in his sacred humanity. By the power of the Holy Spirit, operative in Christ's Church, the saving grace of Christ's death and resurrection is made efficacious for our salvation, making us sons of God, in God's only Son.

We are not Christians merely because our baptism is registered in the parish archives. What really makes us Christians is our incorporation into the body of Christ, our life in Christ through baptism and the Holy Spirit's sanctifying action. Our life of union with God in Christ through the Holy Spirit is the essential, invisible dimension of our church life and it is also the principal effect of the Holy Eucharist in our soul. The visible, institutional Church, however, is the normal means making these riches available.

Vatican II (LG, no. 8) points out that the twofold nature of the Church as an institution and as an event, is grounded on the event of the Incarnation itself. "By a significant analogy, the Church is likened to the mystery of the Incarnate Word. The nature taken by the divine Word serves as the organ of salvation in a union with him that is indissoluble; so also the social framework of the Church serves the Spirit of Christ, the vivifier of Christ's growing body (Ep 4:16). Christ, the sole mediator, in founding and giving unfailing support to his holy Church has made her visible structure the dispenser of the grace and truth which he sheds over all mankind." The mediating role of Christ's humanity, our only access to God, continues in the visible Church which is also inseparably the invisible body of Christ.

God's providence has always dealt with us mercifully in human, earthly forms, taking into account the limitations of our human nature. The Old Testament featured the visible institutions of Israel: law, sacrifices, ark of the covenant, temple of Jerusalem. The Incarnation of God's Son was the pivotal point of God's self-revelation to mankind, the most important happening of all times. Now, until Christ's return in glory, it is the time of the Church, a visible society in which we hear again the words of eternal life and especially participate in visible rites, making available to us and operative in us, the grace of Christ's death and resurrection. Our invisible union together with God in Christ is signified and effected by the visible, juridical society of Christ's Church here below. The Church is not only an instrument of salvation, it is also the event of salvation realized in the world.

The center and summit of all the saving activity of the Church is the celebration of the Eucharist. The heavenly saving action of Christ by the Eucharist erupts on the plane of history in a visible and tangible manner. Christ was lifted up on the cross (Jn 3:13), then to the right hand of his Father (Mk 16:19) where in glory he is living for ever to intercede for us (Heb 7:25). By means of the visible forms of the sacrament of the Eucharist, Christ makes himself really present, he, our glorious savior, drawing all men of all time to himself, and presenting with them in earthly forms his eternal saving worship of his Father.

Already in the Acts of the Apostles (2:42) four elements are very closely linked together: an assembly, the Apostles' preaching, prayer, and the Eucharistic breaking of the bread. A very evident characteristic of the celebration of the Eucharist is that it is an *assembly of the faithful,* a coming together which is far more than a practical necessity, since it is already an effective sign or symbol of the very mystery of the Church. The biblical word for Church, in fact, means the gathering of God's people.

Israel was God's people because of the covenants God made with them. The Church is God's new people gathered together in Christ who in his blood, at the Last Supper and on the Cross ratified the New Covenant, now constantly effective in the Eucharistic celebration.

Israel of old celebrated the day of the Covenant (Dt 18:16) when they gathered together to pledge themselves again to be his people through the observance of the covenant. So now, the Israel of God (Gal 6:16) gathered together to celebrate the Eucharist not only recalls and ratifies, but sacramentally represents the new covenant by which it lives and grows.

The visible congregation gathered for the celebration of the

Eucharist renews in mystery the new covenant and is thus consti-
tuted God's people in the invisible life of Christ and the unity of
the Holy Spirit. The Eucharist is the new covenant, the event
of salvation par excellence, building up the Church as the body of
Christ and the very temple of God.

The liturgy of the Mass is filled with the consciousness of
being the prayer of God's gathered people, joined together in
unity and fellowship. We unite ourselves in spirit with all God's
people, the local bishop and the leader of Christ's whole Church,
the living and the dead, the apostles, the saints, and the martyrs,
the Old Testament types of Christ, the high priest, Abel, Abraham,
and Melchisedech. The repeated Eucharistic gatherings manifest
and effect the reality, unity and identity of Christ's Church
throughout the ages until the Lord comes.

The Church is also the community which Christ has *gathered*
to *worship* the Father in spirit and in truth. Now the celebration
of the Eucharist is the most perfect act of worship of God's
people. The raison d'etre both of the Church and of the Eucharist
is ultimately one thing only: worship offered to God. We can
offer worship because we are God's people; and we become ever
more perfectly his people by offering this Eucharistic sacrifice
of worship and atonement.

The Church as a *community of believers* also finds in the
Eucharistic liturgy its manifestation and effective realization.
From the very beginning celebration of the Eucharist was accompanied by the preaching of the word (Ac 2:42). It is the living
bread of God's word received by faith which prepares the congregation to receive the living bread of Christ's flesh given for
the life of the world (Jn 6). And Christian apostolate is animated
by and directed to the holy liturgy of the Mass.

The Church is above all the *mystical body* of Christ. Now the
heart of the Eucharistic mystery is the body and blood of Christ.
And it is through the celebration of the Eucharist that the visible
society of the Church becomes the mystical body of Christ.

It is through the Eucharistic body of Christ that the mystical
body, the Church, is built up and made one. "Because the bread
is one, we who are many are one body, for we all partake of the

one bread" (1 Cor 10:17). Through the Eucharist we are made one with Christ and thus made one with each other in the fellowship of the one Spirit (Ep 4:4). And the Church which celebrates the Eucharist is itself built up by the Eucharist and finds in the Eucharist its perfect consummation. The theology of the Church is dominated by one over-arching conception, the conception of the Church as a reality of the sacramental order, the mystical body of Christ, preserved and nourished by the sacrament of the Lord's body and blood.

In the words of Vatican II (LG, no. 26): "the mystery of the Lord's Supper is celebrated in order that by the flesh and blood of the Lord's body, the whole brotherhood may be joined together." The community gathered around the altar, under the sacred ministry of the bishop, manifests symbolically that charity and unity of the mystical body without which salvation is impossible. Christ is present in these communities and by his power the one, holy, catholic, and apostolic Church is drawn together; for the precise effect of partaking of Christ's body and blood is transformation into what we receive.

Finally, the eschatological character of the Church as a *pilgrim people* without a lasting city here below (Heb 13:14) is also made manifest in the Eucharist which is our viaticum, the food sustaining us on our journey to the kingdom of heaven. The Eucharist is an anticipation and prefiguring of the great banquet which we hope to share with Christ in God's heavenly glory. It was Christ's pasch (Lk 22:15-18), his passage to his Father. It is also ours because it gives us the pledge of future glory (Jn 6:54). The celebration of the Eucharist, especially on Sunday, the Lord's day, prefigures, anticipates, and brings us closer to the eschatological day of the Lord (1 Cor 1:6; Rv 6:17).

It should then clearly appear that as the Encyclical *Mystici Corporis* (no. 63) puts it: "Like body and soul in us, the Eucharist and the Church are complementary and perfect each other, both having their origin and life in one and the same Savior." By the Eucharist the Church is most fully and perfectly itself, the people of God, the community of worshipping believers, the body of Christ, the heavenly city, the new Jerusalem.

Sixteen

THE EUCHARIST AND THE LIVING CHURCH

Today, paradoxically, as sacramental practice is in ebb tide, and as religion is severely criticized when it is not completely discarded, never has the Eucharist had so much importance in the life of the Church. Not only has it become practically the only act of public prayer in our Churches, but it clearly appears as the point of separation between diverging Christian groups, as is shown by recent Protestant/Catholic statements, and also as the object of urgent desire on the part of those who are deprived of it, such as divorced people or those living in invalid marriages. The Eucharist and religious practice appear as practically inseparable, and no wonder since religious experience is essentially an encounter with God through Christ.

The ecclesial aspect of the Eucharist is not merely one of its values or its distinctive characters such as communion or sacrifice; it is the very heart beat of the Mass. Thus correspondence between the Church and the Eucharist appears in the rites of the Mass, such as the kiss of peace and the sharing of the one bread (1 Cor 10:17); in the public and unique character of the Eucharistic celebration; and, finally, in the end or purpose of the sacrament which is the building up of Christ's mystical body. These links are so close that Eucharistic communion and ecclesial communion are mutually inclusive, overlie, are both the way and the condition of each other. Hence every serious deviation from the profession of one's faith or the conduct of one's life is a betrayal of the Eucharist and subject to excommunication, both in the literal sense of exclusion from the sacraments and in the technical sense of canon, Church law.

The book of Acts (2:42) shows the early Christian community as a brotherhood built up by the teaching of the apostles, the pooling of resources, and the celebration of the Eucharist, the basic Christian prayer described as the sharing, the breaking of the Eucharistic bread. And Paul in 1 Cor 11:23-27 insists that any disorder in the Eucharistic assembly reveals an ecclesial failure, a fraternal failing which falsifies the celebration of the Lord's Supper. And just as the authenticity of the Christian life and of the Eucharist are closely interdependent, so also are ecclesial faith and faith in the Eucharist. In fact, long before the Creed was introduced into the Mass, the Eucharistic anaphoras appear as a profession of faith. A fine example is found in the fourth Eucharistic prayer of our new rite for Mass; it stresses the Trinitarian dimension of the history of salvation along with the Christological dimension, as well as the link between creation and salvation.

This intimate link between the Eucharist and the Church must be well understood. It does not in any way refer to a *fait accompli* but to a goal; we must become what we figure in anticipation in the Eucharist. Neither does it mean that the Church is realized, is brought into concrete existence in the Eucharistic celebration. The Eucharist is the sign and source of the Church's mission to all men, a mission whose actual accomplishment is a gauge of the value of our Eucharists which in turn serve as a criterion of our faith, our union with Christ, and of the genuine character of our action in the world.

This link at the same time theoretical and practical, traditional, very actual and real, between the Eucharist and the Church represents at the same time a great hope for our time, as well as a great need for truth, authenticity, not only in the forms and reality of our faith, but also in its ecclesial and human foundation.

Is there any hope for the Christian Church in our time? Is there any future in being a Christian? What is a Christian? Today we live in a secularized world in which our Christianity is invested in the framewok of our earthly life (for example, in the sense given to marriage and family life) and finds its realization in hopes which are characteristic of all mankind (for example, justice and brotherly love). Yet the Christian can find in the Eucharistic celebration a privileged occasion for self identification, and this not only in the specific liturgical acts but also and especially in their attestation of all the dimensions of the Christian faith as an answer to the call and the love of God in Christ.

In the celebration of the Church's Eucharist, I measure my faith against that of the Church throughout the centuries, the liturgy being a refraction of the apostolic faith, as St. Paul himself testified to the Corinthians (1 Cor 11:23, "What I have received, I in turn pass on to you"). As a negative corroboration, it may be pointed out that the Fathers of the Church also felt and showed the correlations which exist between Christological-ecclesial and Eucharistic errors.

What is true of the faith of the community is also true of the profession of that faith before men. What we profess we should live by, and granting that our faith is essentially a faith in the humanity of Christ given as gift to men, it must include a truly human experience of this faith, in an assembly which is authentically human, and in signs which are truly meaningful and significant. The itinerary of faith from the gospel preaching to the Eucharistic celebration will be a long process but should progress from one human experience to another until the goal is finally reached.

The Eucharist, in particular, will solve the problem of Christian prayer. For many Christians today the celebration of the Eucharist is their only experience of prayer. Personal, private prayer surely represents a type of prayer which communal worship will never be able to replace competely. Yet it is no secret that it offers to many modern Christians practically insurmountable difficulties. Certain ancient forms or methods of prayer are now wholly unacceptable or need much critical review; one must also contend with the rhythms of modern life, the investments made to other aspects of our existence in faith, the lack of formation or even of stimulation offered by pastors. These are reasons why solitary prayer is nearly impossible for the average Christian; and for other reasons even for religious and priests choral and even regular prayer have their own problems. On the other hand since most Christians want to live by the Eucharist, the Eucharistic celebration could be the means of fostering personal, interior prayer, by helping them little by little to understand the bearing and consequences of the words they hear and pronounce, and of the symbolic actions they perform. It is surely important that the fundamental dimension of the Christian experience, involved in personal, private prayer, be truly realized somewhere in a Christian's life, and the celebration of the Eucharist appears as an ideal center for this operation.

One aspect of the Eucharist needs special attention if our celebration is to become a more attractive human experience. Some of the actual disaffection for the Eucharist might be dispelled if our celebration became really a celebration by reviving its joyful, festive character. The Eucharist, in fact, is the memorial and actualization of an historical event which is meant to transform human history, the Paschal mystery, the death and resurrection of Christ which are inseparable elements of the mystery of our redemption and salvation. Its purpose is to join together actual joy and hope, union with God, with responsibility in this, his world. An antinomy between this festive spirit and the moral obligation still marks our Catholic cultic life. Granting that there are natural rhythms in life, especially for feasts, and also the needs and exigencies of fidelity, yet our essential motivation in Church attendance should be marked by the themes of need, attraction, and freedom, and not of obligation and sanction. Our Sunday Mass should be a joyful occasion and not a mere mass manifestation or joyless performance of a medicinal operation, granting that the mystery of redemption is serious business, and that the way of the Cross, the narrow path which leads to salvation (Mt 7:14) is not a bed of roses.

Another ecclesial problem where again the Eucharist appears as the touchstone of the life of the Church is the question of active participation and of the responsibility of all the community in the Eucharistic celebration. We can only say briefly here that the essential meaning or fruit of the Eucharistic sacrament will give the solution to the many questions which crop up here. Should we share the same Eucharist in spite of our tensions and divisions, which are not only political and social but deeply personal, and

in any case a real part of our lives? This brings up the question
of legitimate diversities and conflicts of interest. The Eucharist
with its ultimate purpose of unifying charity is perhaps the privileged place to learn how to carry together disagreements, especially when one considers the distance which exists between a
certain indispensable unity of intention and the indefinite diversity of possible opinions and solutions, not only theoretically but
also practically in every phase of our actual life.

It is clear that if the Church, the body of Christ is not first of
all *us*, it does not exist at all. We are the ones who celebrate the
Eucharist in union with Christ and his priest, and not some vague
juridical entity or some mythical personage who would be acting
in our name. This consideration throws new light on the identity
which we assert between the Eucharist and the Church, and at the
same time it underscores some basic consequences. Only a Christian
community professing effectively the same faith, living and attest-
ing the same love, and sharing the same hope can be the Church
which celebrates the Eucharist. Sinners, no doubt, people seeking
and not always sure of their faith; but still God's people at large
and not an elite club. At the same time, however, the Eucharist
is not simply a human act but a mystery of grace, symbolically
but effectively available, a reality in our world very apt to signify
God's plan which it realizes, and where God's love reaches down
to us, transforms us, and reunites us. It is the Church of all times
and all places which is made actual in our Eucharistic celebration
because of our union with our bishop and the local Church, and
with the other authorities, especially the pope and the universal
Church.

Another consequence is insistence on the human character
of the Christian community. Although faith brings us together,
the fact remains that there can be no real Christian community
without men and women living a human life and witnessing
to Christ in our time. The Church must be a human community
before being a Christian community; a community of men,
who are worthy of their name by helping others to realize
their manhood and their human condition, especially the outcast, the poor, the suffering, and the needy. We must first of

all translate the hope of the kingdom of God in projects of earthly justice, beneficence, and fraternity; people must first be humanized before they can be Christianized. The Christian experience involves the whole of human life and existence. An ancient philosopher stated that because he was a man there is nothing human in which he should not be involved. Being a Christian does not abrogate this basic human obligation.

The practical problems involved in unifying our human condition in the actual celebration of the Eucharist are many and complex. There are, for example, the disagreements of political parties which in no way should violate Christian unity. Some other differences of opinion can be more radical and lead, for example, to legal conflicts, yet even then there is always possible a basic belief in the other person's good faith and openness to dialogue. The question of war is more complicated.

Our Eucharistic communion will be authentic only if we give the world a full and true interpretation of Christ's gospel. The Eucharistic celebration is the ecclesial and human foundation, source, and ultimate realization of our Christian faith.

Seventeen

THE EUCHARISTIC ASSEMBLY

The Acts of the Apostles, in the description of the early Christian community, feature the breaking of the Eucharistic bread as a characteristic of the early Christian Church (2:42). The Eucharistic assembly is, in fact, the major assembly of the Christian people, in which the people of God find their deepest meaning and greatest effectiveness.

It is an assembly entirely based on faith. Now by definition the Eucharist is the mystery of faith; and without faith, which is man's free response to God's revelation, there is no effective Eucharistic assembly. Faith in Christ's commandment, "do this in memory of me": Christians know their Lord's command, obey it, accomplish it in love. Faith in God's word in Christ: the Christian hears God's word, is converted by the power of the word, and is nourished by the word which like the Eucharist is the bread of life. Faith in the presence of Christ: Christians adore Christ present in the Eucharist and in so doing gather around Christ who becomes their rallying center; they adore with Christ who is the only priest offering his sacrifice, and in Christ whose sacrifice unites them to himself by the Spirit's interior grace and to each other in common love of God. Faith active in love is then the first force exerted in the Christian Eucharistic assembly.

This assembly shapes the Christian community. A human community is never found perfectly formed from the outset. Founded on juridical bonds, on reason and justice, the community is shaped above all by the bonds of fellowship and love which must constantly be renewed in full liberty. Christian fellowship is the meaning and the immediate purpose of the Eucharistic assembly. It is inculcated by a spiritual movement of adoration and love which should be the essential trait of an authentic celebration.

The Christian community is a community of conversion, built on repentant love. This is a natural, normal dimension since it is always as sinner that man approaches Christ's sacrifice to convert himself to the true and living God and obtain his pardon through Jesus Christ. Hence the penitential service at the beginning of Mass and the recognition of one's misery before receiving holy communion.

It is also a community of adoring love, of adoration in spirit and in truth inspired by the Holy Spirit. The Eucharistic prayer actually is a benediction, a blessing, that is, adoration, praise, thanksgiving, supplication by Christ who died, rose again, and now sends us his Spirit.

The Christian community is a community of fraternal love which brings the assembly together, a holy community where there is no longer Greek or Jew, slave or freedman, but simply children of God. This will be the work of conversion: to forgive, to welcome, to discard aggressiveness, break down the barriers of egoism, and decide to serve. Witnessing also builds up the community. We assemble for others as well as for ourselves, mutually strengthening one another in God's service, without forgetting beneficence, the care of the poor which always had a place of honor in the Eucharistic assembly (1 Cor 11). The Eucharist is the fraternal meal which builds up and knits closely the Christian community. We are nourished by Christ, the Savior of the world, the head which draws together the whole Christian body, communicating his power of cohesion and unity. Already a natural meal has the biological purpose of sustaining life, the sociological effect of renewing human ties, and the religious sense of blessing God for all his gifts; over and above all this the Eucharistic meal is infinitely richer because it has also the characteristics of a sacrifice. It is a meal of healing, the remedy for sins because the Son who was sent "to be a bodily and spiritual medicine" (SC, no. 5) is always present. It is a meal of divinization because it infuses deeply into our being the life of Christ, his Trinitarian life (Jn 6:57); because it unites us to Christ who comes to make us love and live God's truth, his love and his will; because it conforms us to Christ Jesus by whom we become "Gods and sons of God" (Ps 81:6). It is a meal of divine fraternity because the Eucharist is a meal of charity, and love builds the Church. The meal must then be characterized by order, consideration for others, and a selfless approach. It unites the faithful who eat the one bread (1 Cor 10:17), the only truly living One in whom we find life.

The Eucharist is also a meal of thanksgiving. If God created food "to be received with thanksgiving by those who believe" (1 Tm 4:3), how much more the divine food, the bread of life and immortality, the bread which unites all believers in him. The Eucharistic sacrifice reaches completion in sacramental communion where we all become one in Christ who constantly gives thanks and glory to his Father who sent him and raised him from the dead as the first fruit of our resurrection. The Eucharist is a meal of resurrection: it confers immortality, it anticipates mysteriously our final resurrection and the eschatological banquet. In short, the Eucharistic meal attains its full result in the other world, in God's glory because it is fulfilled in Jesus Christ who is himself the beyond and the glory. "He who eats my flesh has eternal life and I will raise him up on the last day" (Jn 6:54).

Finally, the Eucharistic assembly is the assembly of God's glory: this is its finality and ultimate signification. The Eucharist exists for God's glory which is realized by the sacrifice, but it must be desired, received, freely accepted by the faithful. The assembly of purification and conversion restores in man the image of Christ, the image of God, and that is the first glory of God. The assembly of prayer, benediction, and supplication, joins in the act of giving glory to God. The assembly of fraternal love completes the image of God: "that they may be one as you and I, Father, are one" (Jn 17:21); it fulfills the redemption of Christ who died to gather together all his sheep. By the Eucharist all our life is directed to God's glory, all our human activities "become spiritual sacrifices, acceptable to God through Jesus Christ. During the celebration of the Eucharist, these sacrifices are most lovingly offered to the Father along with the Lord's body" (LG, no. 34).

Christ is the rock foundation of the Christian assembly which is entirely founded by him and on him. It finds in him its first principle of existence. It is an assembly of baptized faithful and the sacramental character of baptism is a participation in the priesthood of Jesus Christ. It follows that all the assembly offers the sacrifice. The Church body of Christ, however, is structured, well organized and it is by the hands and the heart of its priests that the sacrifice is offered to God: "acting in the person of Christ and proclaiming his mystery they join the offering of the faithful to the sacrifice of their Head, rendering present the one sacrifice of the New Testament" (LG, no. 28).

This is how Christ is the principle of unity in the Christian community. Faithful to Christ's order, interpreted by his Church, the community assembles as it did from the highest antiquity. The center of the community is Christ, represented visibly by the bishop or the priest who participate "on their level of ministry in the function of Christ, the sole mediator" (LG, no. 28). It is Christ invisibly by the interior grace which derives from him, a theological grace of faith, hope and charity. It is Christ sacramentally who in the Eucharist is present in person, adored, praised and blessed by the community as its Lord and Spouse. Thus Christ is the final result and end of the Eucharistic assembly by his actual presence and action in which are present the past mystery of the Cross-Resurrection, the actual mystery of the assembly of salvation, and the future mystery of the eschatological assembly at the time of the Parousia.

The presence of Christ is a presence in mystery but at the same time a presence which is deeply personal. It is the presence of Christ such as he is in heaven, the eternal, incarnate Word, dead but risen from the dead: "I am the first and the last, the living one. I was dead and now I am to live forever and ever, and I hold the keys of death and Hades" (Rv 1:17-18). Precisely because Christ himself is present in the Eucharist, his redemptive act is present with all its dynamism and all its efficacy. Redemption is actualized by the presence and the action of the Redeemer himself, the Son of God made man, in his eternal act of redemption. And this presence transforms completely the Christian assembly, which finds in the incarnate Christ present in person its full realization.

It thus becomes a transcendent, mystery-assembly since its source, its essence and existence as well as its end are God himself made man. It consequently experiences an extraordinary reversal. It begins by calling on Christ, singing to him and supplicating, but Christ takes over the assembly in person and it is in his offering that the assembly is reformed, perfected and offered to the Father. Incorporated from above in Christ's redemptive act, it becomes an assembly of perfect adoration, thanksgiving, and supplication, infinitely surpassing the poor mortals by whom and in whom it is realized.

Notwithstanding its human limitations the Eucharistic assembly always opens a universal horizon. Every time Mass is celebrated the whole Church is involved and each assembly represents the entire Church present in its head. If each individual celebration of the Eucharist is local, the local Church is a happening which involves the universal Church. And furthermore, the whole Church in all its states finds itself gathered and assembled in the Eucharistic community: the militant Church, the community of salvation and redemption on pilgrimage here below; the suffering Church undergoing its final purification and officially remembered in the Eucharistic prayer; and the Church triumphant invoked on earth and united in heaven to its Lord's constant intercession (Heb 7:25).

Finally, all humanity is present at the Eucharist which extends the virtue of its mercy to all men who potentially are members of Jesus Christ, and hence of the Church, since they are all called and redeemed by our Lord. "I pray not only for these but for all who through their word will believe in me" (Jn 17:20). "I have other sheep that are not of this fold and these I have to lead as well. They too will listen to my voice" (Jn 10:16). This is the universal dimension of Christ's redemption and consequently of the Eucharist: "This is my body given for you . . . my blood shed for you and for all men."

The Christian assembly gathered around the Eucharistic altar effects in time the presence of eternity, the eternity of Jesus, our

Lord, transforming our time into a time of salvation, not of condemnation; of divine life, not of death; of growth, not of inanition; of glory, not of annihilation.

Christ is the Alpha and the Omega, the beginning and the end. In a sense, here below, this is also true of the Eucharist. The Eucharistic assembly is the source and the summit of the Christian mission, of apostolic work (SC, no. 10). As Christ passed from the Last Supper to the Cross and Resurrection, so also must the Church go from the Eucharist to the work of world redemption. As the Christian people are assembled and renewed by the Eucharist, they receive the agape, the apostolic love which creates and recreates man, redeems him and saves him.

The Eucharist is thus an impulse towards the fulfillment of God's kingdom, an assembly in hope. "Every time you eat this bread and drink this cup, you proclaim the Lord's death until he comes" (1 Cor 11:26). The Church is a pilgrim Church waiting for the final coming of its glorious Lord and the total transfiguration of all its members. The Eucharistic memorial of the past sufferings of our Lord, in a sense gives way before the prefiguration of our future glory. There is no longer need of a souvenir when Christ is present in the fulness of his glorious state, when all the figures have been accomplished. In the Eucharist we expect in sure hope, the perfect community when God will be all in all (1 Cor 15:28). Thus the pilgrim sacrifice is a figure, an anticipation of the consummated heavenly sacrifice. By means of this effective symbol we are drawn on high by Christ, sanctified by him, incorporated and unified in him. The Eucharist is truly the Christian Passover, the effective passage from this world to the heavenly Father.

The Eucharist is the active, effective hope of the new covenant, giving us the substance of all our true desires, namely, the glory of God and the salvation of men. It demands the full exercise of our human liberty, and in this sense the Eucharist is a task which is accomplished, in line with its nature as a memorial of the cross of Christ, by what may be called our Messianic sufferings. There are always obstacles to the kingdom, battles to be won, our death to be overcome. Our results are always provisory; our human liberty is never totally converted or fixed in goodness, hence the need for evangelical patience (Lk 21:19).

Our Christian task, however, is also accomplished in the life of the resurrection with a share in the Messianic joys, in communion with Christ. A Christian's life of consecration to the work of Christ, his sufferings and even his death are transfigured in contact with the victorious Christ. This paradox of suffering and joy is the very paradox of hope in Jesus Christ.

In hope we are already saved (Rm 8:24). The Eucharist, mystery of the dead and risen Christ, is the source of this hope, a hope that cannot fail us since it is especially by the Eucharist that "the love of God has been poured into our hearts by the Holy Spirit who has been given to us" (Rm 5:5).

Eighteen

THE EUCHARIST AND THE HOLY SPIRIT

Our generation is blessed with a special grace of renewed attraction for the Holy Spirit. Our return to the biblical sources, to the Fathers, and to the ancient liturgies is really a return to the spirit of the Scriptures, the spirit of tradition, the spirit of the liturgy. This focus on the origins draws our attention in a special way to the Holy Spirit who enlightens, pacifies, and unifies the Church, the body of Christ.

The mystery of the Holy Spirit is really unfathomable, like the mystery of God himself. Even after revelation, the divine trinity remains transcendent, completely other, dwelling in light inaccessible (1 Tm 6:16). This is true even of the Incarnate Word, the divine person of revelation par excellence, the image of the eternal God. Yet by definition, the mystery of Christ is a mystery of revelation, of Incarnation, of the Word that is uttered, that resounds and penetrates into history, into time and space, takes forms, is accessible to the senses, to sight and hearing, and is the object of experience as well as intellectual understanding.

Who has ever seen or heard the Spirit of God? The Spirit penetrates and plumbs the depths of God, is an inherent part of the unfathomable mystery and of the eternal plenitude of the divine trinity, yet at the same time he establishes in man's heart an inalienable divine presence, a reality which at the same time fulfills and overreaches man's being. The Holy Spirit is a present reality but remains irreducible, impalpable, simple yet also multiple and varied in its operations; he blends with the deepest inwardness of man, with the ultimate roots of our personality, yet remains the completely-other, an inspiration, an impulse, a flame, a supernatural eruption into our life.

There is a diversity of manifestations of the Holy Spirit in the life of the Church and consequently a plurality of authentic and complementary experiences of the presence of the Spirit in us.

There is first a general presence of the Holy Spirit diffused, undetermined, a vital impulse, biological, cosmic, natural in character: a thirst for truth, a quest for the absolute or for simple justice, a sense of beauty. This presence underlies all esthetic and religious experience, all creative effort, all true encounter, all overreaching beyond our proper limitations. All this involves an implicit, hidden, previous action where one could recognize the presence of the Spirit or of the Logos who enlightens every man; a presence which determines the inspiring intention, the creative energy, constitutes a factor at once of diversification, of specification, of personal property, but also of unification, of assembly, of solidarity, and of human communion at all levels.

If Christians may legitimately specify the identity of this vital impulse and recognize it as a divine inspiration, as the work and mark of divine providence, it is not necessary, or often advisable, to institutionalize or define the action, often incognito, of God's Spirit, by an official recognition or an ecclesial appropriation of the work of him who remains master of his gifts and free not to limit his inspiration. The beauty and fervor of the first love is seldom recaptured. Yet in the long run, there is a deep, remarkable convergence between Christian revelation and the slow maturing of humanity, its search for authenticity, even if historical Christianity can set itself up as a screen, as an opaque curtain, impeding the identification of these diffused energies or even stifling the biblical spirit (Is 42:3).

In the light of Christ's revelation, the Holy Spirit takes on a much more concrete and personal meaning, although even here some distinctions must be made. Already in the Old Testament preparation and also in the evangelical realization, and in the time of the Church, the Holy Spirit is inseparable from the Word of God, the Incarnate Word, and the Church, Christ's body. This firm relation of the Spirit with the Son of God manifested in Jesus Christ constitutes one of the fundamental themes of Trinitarian theology and of all Christian revelation, and determines also all the life and structures of the Church. Now, in the interior of these three moments of divine revelation in the world (Old Testament, Incarnation, Church) it is possible to distinguish three specific modes of relation of the Holy Spirit to the Word of God: maturation, manifestation, expansion.

From the beginning the Spirit of God appears at work in the slow and mysterious process of creation, brooding over and vivifying the primeval waters, infusing the seeds of life, warming the inert primary matter. In the emergence of man it is again the Spirit who infuses man's vital energy, incarnates in him the image of God, and thus leads him to filial obedience to the Father.

At the time of the fall and of the consequent salvation history, the Spirit of God is that mysterious inner voice that untiringly calls man back to his sinless origin and reminds him of his destiny. All the history of Israel is already a slow divine pedagogy. The Holy Spirit inspires the prophets and strengthens them in their testimony for the word of God; it assures a slow fermentation of their preaching, leading up to maturation and a more and more impatient and painful expectation of the Savior and Messianic times.

At the time of the Incarnation, the Holy Spirit is the Spirit of the Incarnation, the one in whom and by whom the divine Word erupts into our human history, the one who prepares a human body as the temple of the Word's divinity. Luke's gospel alone describes the intellectual and spiritual growth of Jesus as an increase in wisdom as well as in stature, and especially in God's favor (Lk 2:40-52), a reference, no doubt, before all else to the presence and action of the Holy Spirit in Christ's human life.

Finally, the work of maturation by the Holy Spirit continues in the life of the Church. The Spirit assembles the people into the Church, prepares them and consecrates them for worship, enlightens them by his inspired word, incarnates this word in the worship, in the preaching as well as in the Eucharist. In the ecclesial community it is the Spirit himself who prays, who invokes in the bottom of our hearts the blessed name of Jesus, who re-echoes in the Eucharistic assembly the maranatha *Come, Lord Jesus* (Rv 22:20).

The Spirit is inseparable from the Word, he manifests its authenticity by interior evidence, he makes it known as true because he animates it, and gives it life. As prophetic word, the inspiration of the sacred authors, the Spirit is the power confirming the people's covenant with God; he is also the interior light giving us the intelligence of the Scriptures and the understanding of God's interventions in history. It is only in the light of the Spirit that profane history is integrated to sacred history and given for an axis divine providence and God's untiring will of life and of salvation.

In evangelical times, Jesus is filled with the Spirit and power of God (Lk 4:14); he presents himself in Galilee as one anointed, consecrated by the Spirit (Lk 4:18); his preaching is gracious, authoritative, powerful, inspiring (Lk 4:22, 32, 35, 36). The gospel narratives constantly accentuate and specify this presence of the Spirit of God in Jesus, in his teaching, and in his works.

The dove at the Jordan comes down from heaven, rests over Jesus, and is part of the Father's testimony. It expresses the eternal relation of the Spirit of God who proceeds from the Father and the Son, abiding in them from and for all eternity. The Holy Spirit is the Spirit of Jesus; he penetrates him, manifests him, and unveils him to the world (Ac 10:38).

The blinding light on Thabor, the unparalleled whiteness of Christ's garments, the cloud, are all symbolic manifestations of the Spirit. From the Incarnation to the Ascension, all Christ's earthly life was a life full of the Holy Spirit, his gifts, his signs, his impulse, and his fire. The Spirit accompanied Christ through the Passion and on the cross, the supreme impoverishment where Jesus realized the ideal of the beatitudes of which he is the great and only true example: "Blessed is the poor in the Spirit, to him belongs the kingdom of heaven." The presence of the Spirit is also that irresistible force which breaks the seals of the empty tomb, the exuberant joy which filled the women and the disciples, the blinding light of the resurrection, a presence that remained with Jesus even in his death and over which the gates of hell were powerless.

In the time of the Church, the Holy Spirit constantly models and builds up the Church as the body of Christ. All the prayer of the Church, the repeated invocations for the coming of the Holy Spirit are the continuation of the fervent prayer of the apostolic community gathered in the upper room in expectation of Pentecost. In him the risen Lord is present to the Church, guides it, and is united to the ecclesial community in the Eucharistic communion.

"Receive the Holy Spirit," our risen Lord told his disciples (Jn 20:22). The gift of Pentecost is the necessary fulfillment of the Paschal mystery. If the Holy Spirit is the one who prepares the coming of Christ, who announces him, reveals him, incarnates him, makes him present to the ecclesial community, it must also be pointed out that in a movement of inverse relation, since Pentecost it is Christ who prays the Father to send the Holy Spirit; it is our Lord who himself sends the Spirit in the name of the Father. Christ in turn becomes the giver of the Spirit and this gift is perpetuated in the life of the Church in a perpetual and permanent Pentecost.

It is in the Eucharistic mystery that the gift of the Holy Spirit is constantly renewed in the Church. The *epiclesis* (invocation) of the Spirit on the assembly and on the Eucharistic elements expresses the total and constant life-situation of the Church: a state of expectation and prayer for the coming of the Spirit; a fullness and a glowing enthusiasm because of the Spirit's vivifying presence; a confession of the name and Lordship of the risen Jesus to the whole world. The missionary and apostolic expansion of the Church is a fundamental aspect of its vocation and presence in the world. The object of this testimony is the presence of the risen Christ whom we adore in the power and light of the Holy Spirit. The dismissal of all the Christian liturgies (go in peace) expresses the constant obedience of the Church to our Lord's commandment: "Go out to the whole world, proclaim the good news to all creation" (Mk 16:15).

The liturgy expresses by the Eucharistic assembly and its dismissal into the world, the profound law and rhythm of the Church which congregates from the four ends of the earth, builds itself up in adoration and communion, then disperses fortified and nourished by the bread of life, moved by the Spirit to witness, preach, and make visible Christ, the only Lord and Master of the Church, the king of the world.

All prayer and witness of the Church are a prayer and a witness in the Spirit by the Spirit; in its prayer the Church identifies itself to the Holy Spirit; it is the Spirit who prays in the very heart of the Church (Rm 8:15-26; Mt 10:20).

At times the Church identifies itself with the bride, prays, cries from its inmost heart, seeks its Spouse, invokes him and seeks to attract him, is totally oriented to him. "Come, Lord Jesus," such is the only testimony of the Spirit; to reveal Christ, to announce him, and make him present. At other times, it is with Christ that the Church is identified by the Holy Spirit, and then it is the prayer of Jesus, the High Priest, that resounds and rises, in the Eucharistic assembly, to the Father, a prayer for unity, life, and salvation, an invocation for the coming of the kingdom in the Holy Spirit in whom converge all the graces, all the charisms, all joy, holiness, strength, power, and love.

In this progress towards the Trinitarian unity, the Holy Spirit reveals himself at the same time as the giver of divine life, as the one who realizes the meeting and the union with Christ Jesus; the friend, the precursor of the bridegroom, who announces him and disappears before him. But at the same time Pentecost reveals the Holy Spirit as a person, and not simply a function, a light, or a power, but a person who bears an ineffable name, inseparable from Christ yet not confused with him, a person greater and beyond his gifts.

Thus Christ is the origin, the goal, the end of the Church; the Spirit, the power of the Resurrection, is the Church's transforming light, the Spirit of unity and of Catholicity in liberty; the Holy Spirit takes constantly closer possession of the members of Christ's body to re-create the world by the power of the Resurrection. Thus the Church implores the Spirit to help her find the way, to be directed like the Son to the Father: "God, Holy Paraclete, who formerly spoke through the prophets, and in our days by the Apostles; Spirit teacher of the little ones, Spirit by whom the

Father is known, by whom we believe in the Son, fill us with the wisdom of your doctrine, enrich us with the knowledge of your mysteries. Let your brightness and your rays shine in us" (Ancient Syrian prayer).

The mystery of the Holy Spirit is a mystery of divine love and unity, for the Holy Spirit is the Creator of unity at all the levels of man's transformation and re-creation. Communion with the Holy Spirit is a multiple, polyvalent reality. Man is reconciled with the Father, in Christ, by the Holy Spirit. Such is the first meaning of Pentecost, the coming of a new relation between man and his Creator, between the prodigal son and his Father. The Spirit also reunifies man interiorly with himself. The supernatural life restores the true hierarchy in man, the true relation between the corporal, psychic, affective, and spiritual levels of his being. By the submission of the body to the soul, of the soul to the Spirit, man radiates the presence of the Holy Spirit within him.

Reconciled with God and reunited with himself, man enters into the communion, the catholicity of the Church; he is incorporated in Christ and consequently with his brothers. A mysterious, indescribable but very real solidarity unites us all in sin, in evil, and in death, but also in salvation, in Christ, by the Church. The Christian receives God's light but must radiate it, not of course like a mere transplant relay. This rediscovery of the other fellow, of human communion, of the face of Christ incognito in our neighbor, especially in the one who suffers, is the missionary dimension of the Apostolic Pentecost, as also of the permanent Pentecost which should mark our Eucharistic celebrations. The Church, between the two comings of Christ, is in a state of mission. This mission, this testimony, is grounded and originates in our personal experience of and encounter with the risen Christ. And the Eucharist is precisely the time and place when, in the light of the Holy Spirit and in communion with him, this Paschal illumination is realized, dispelling all darkness.

The work of salvation wrought by Christ is a work of unity. The Church subsists, in spite of disruptive forces, by the power of Christ's prayer (Jn 17) by which it is maintained in unity and preserved in truth, holiness and glory, that is, in the Spirit of the Father: "And I will pray the Father and he will give you another Paraclete, to be with you forever" (Jn 14:16).

Nineteen

THE EUCHARISTIC CELEBRATION

Celebration of life is today a popular trend, secular or sacred. Our philosophy or theology of hope has the same theme: life is worth living. Our fight against war, poverty, and disease, our stand for the freedom of the human spirit, even the prevalent use of drugs, all represent a search for enjoyment which is clearly the logic of living. The joys of the spirit are not the only commendable pleasures. We must recover the celebration character of our total human existence; our life must be lived on this earth, and we cannot be asked to repudiate the functions of our human body. "God saw everything which he had made and indeed it was very good" (Gn 1:31). God also finds joy in recovering what was lost (Lk 15:7, 10). The forgiveness of sins is the power to receive God and rejoice in his presence in union with Christ. Briefly, the Eucharist, "the blood of the covenant poured for the forgiveness of sins" (Mt 26:28), is par excellence our God-given means to celebrate: the sacrament of promise, hope, and joy.

To eat, drink, and be merry suggest an Epicurean, hedonist philosophy of life, a style of living which seems to be condemned in the gospel (Lk 12:15-20). But on closer examination what is rejected in the Lucan parable of the "Rich Fool" is not the enjoyment of life, already approved in the Old Testament (Ec 3:12-13, 22, 9:7-10), but the misfortune of not being "rich in the sight of God" (Lk 12:20). Our Lord himself believed that life should be enjoyed; he was accused of being a winebibber (Mt 11:19) when actually he saw that man should be able to celebrate God and rejoice in all his gifts. Christ came to be with us and to feed us the Bread of life; daily bread but also the promise of the future in the forgiveness of our sins, peace and joy, the community and fellowship of the Church in the Holy Spirit. We eat, drink, and are merry not because tomorrow we die, but because we live today in the hope of an eternal life we already possess (Jn 6:54).

St. Paul stated: "Everything created by God is good and nothing is to be rejected provided it is received with thanksgiving" (1 Tm 4:14). Our problem today is not so much that we lack anything but that we have everything and are enjoying it less. We are not Eucharistic people, we do not find our joy in God, which is what thanksgiving (Eucharist) is. We do not know genuine celebration, we have no real thanksgiving.

Our Lord was a Eucharistic person. He "ate and drank" (Mt 11:18). He did not despise basic human satisfactions but enjoyed our earthly life. He was always eating and drinking with somebody, breaking bread and giving thanks (Mt 14:19), blessing the common use of ordinary things. The richest heritage he left us is the Eucharistic meal, a supper in common which signifies and effects communion with God and fellowship with one another. The Lord's Supper is an affirmation of life in Christ's death, a celebration of the Paschal mystery, of that life we have with God through Christ's death on the Cross and his glorious resurrection, a life made available to us by his forgiving presence (Rv 5:6; Heb 7:25); a life which ultimately involves enjoyment of the body as much as of the soul. "Anyone who eats my flesh and drinks my blood has eternal life and I shall raise him up on the last day" (Jn 6:54).

Paul was another one of those Eucharistic people who enjoy life. For him as for Christ a wedding banquet and the sexual union of man and woman were symbols of excitement and enjoyment of life with God. In the Old Testament the symbol of Israel as the wife of Yahweh is common (Ho 1:2). Jesus speaks of the Messianic age as a time of wedding (Mt 22:1-14, 25:1-13), and for Paul Christian marriage is a symbol of Christ's union with his Church (Ep 5:25-33). Thus the prophetic image of earlier days is sanctioned and applied to the new Israel of God (Gal 6:16).

We also must be Eucharistic people finding our joy in God and not in anything less than God. The word Eucharist is the transliteration of a Greek word which means to rejoice, bless, give thanks. It is a term which is associated with a celebration, a feast, a festival, and clearly suggests how the first Christians thought of our Lord's Last Supper: as a thanksgiving, a memorial and celebration of God's wonderful saving deeds in our behalf. Have we lost this dimension of the Eucharistic mystery? The Eucharist is a sacrifice and a cultural exercise but also a celebration of the mystery of our salvation and a joyful anticipation of its full possession. It brings our lives into the very presence of Christ and helps us find God's blessing in Christ upon our entire earthly day-to-day existence.

"Whatever you do in word or deed, do everything in the name of the Lord Jesus, giving thanks to God the Father through him" (Col 3:17). Thanksgiving to God in all things, in every circumstance and situation in our life is what makes our life truly worthwhile. But this is not possible without Christ who makes God real to us, but also makes us real, truly human beings. It is he whom we meet in the breaking of the bread (Lk 24:35); he is the one we love and share in the Supper. God gives us Christ and we respond in thanksgiving, in acts of praise and joy; we become truly human, loving God and loving God's people, "thanksgiving" in unity and harmony with all things and all people because of Jesus Christ.

When St. Paul told the Corinthians, "Christ, our Passover, has been sacrificed, let us therefore celebrate the feast . . . with the unleavened bread of sincerity and truth" (1 Cor 5:8), he clearly had the Eucharist as the backdrop of his exhortation. The Christian must be united to the sacrificed and risen Christ in an unending Passover. The Christian's life must be, as it were, an unending Eucharistic celebration. Christ does not die anymore; the victory is ours. Our Lord lives with the power to save, and no matter how hopeless things may seem, life can still be a festival, a victory celebration. Christians gather round the altar because they believe that life is worth celebrating. The liturgy constantly suggests this theme of celebration: "Lift up your hearts!" "Holy, Holy, Holy!" "Do this in remembrance of me!" "Let us proclaim the mystery of faith!" "The peace of the Lord be with you always." As we come to eat and drink the body and blood of the risen Christ, we look up and ahead. Our past is behind and our future before us. We live in the presence of Christ who is the Lamb of God, our forgiveness, our life and salvation. The time is less for commiserating than for celebrating, for the expression of joy rather than sorrow and contrition. Above everything else eating and drinking with Christ and our fellow Christians is a free, a festive occasion. God and his Christ love us (Jn 3:16; Rv 1:5); our Lord is now alive to bless us (Heb 7:25). Here is our opportunity to relive and celebrate the highlights of the history of our salvation, to renew our Christian commitment, and to anticipate the joyful hope of our salvation.

Today the importance of the individual, of each man's dignity and freedom before God, is more than ever considered. True individuality and identity, however, are impossible apart from community. Everyone needs meaningful supportive experiences; participation is the way to individual strength. Now within the community of Christ's Church the eating and drinking of his Supper is the foundation stone of all participation. "Because the bread is one, though there are many of us, we form a single body, for we all share in the same bread" (1 Cor 10:17). The purpose of the sacrament is the building up of the Body of Christ. "Now you are the body of Christ and individually members of it" (1 Cor 12:27); "Individually members of one another" (Rm 12:5). The body cannot exist without its members, and the individual member is nothing without the body. At the same time there is no danger of losing one's individuality within the community.

Paul's approach to the Eucharist and fellowship is very concrete and practical. What the Corinthians (1 Cor 11:17-34) failed to understand was that at the Lord's Table, Christians become what they eat. As a member of the body of Christ, the Christian becomes one with Christ and all the other members; he participates in the fellowship and communion of the saints. He cannot be unmindful of the needs of his brothers and of the whole community.

Something happens when we share in the Eucharistic meal. We recognize one another as brothers; we grow in love and concern for each other. Our feeding on the bread of life contributes to the healing of the body of Christ, to its necessary renewal and growth. The Lord's Supper cannot be merely a private communion within a public setting, otherwise we would be like a citizen who is concerned only with his own rights. We must be people who need people. We cannot live with blinders on, seeing only our own needs.

Eating and drinking the Eucharist means participation, Christ participating in our lives and we participating in his. Identification with Christ and his Church restores us to a healthy regard for self; it lifts us out of our isolation and loneliness and gives us a sense of belonging. In the Eucharist the many become one, the lost find a home, the sufferer comfort and rest; the individual discovers himself in the living Christ, and the community of the Church moves toward fulfillment as the body of Christ.

This idea of fulfillment brings up another problem: the search for meaning, identity, purpose, authenticity. Here again our Eucharistic eating and drinking provides the answer. If a man has a *why* for his life he can bear with almost any *how*. The Eucharist provides a sense of anticipation and hope which enables us to keep on going in our life struggle. "As often as you eat this bread and drink this cup you proclaim the Lord's death until he comes" (1 Cor 11:26). In the Eucharist the living Christ leads his Church to the ultimate healing of the resurrection. As we look back to our Lord's death and resurrection, we anticipate in hope his return in glory at the Parousia.

The Eucharistic mystery is actually three-dimensional. It is first of all a celebration in the present which gives us the living Christ. But the one who lives with us and for us is the Lord who died. Out of the past comes the power of his death. In the sacrament we experience his mighty death and resurrection as he brings his risen life to bear upon ours. And all this "until he comes." Our Lord invites us to participate with him in the meal which proclaims his present power and his future glory. As we eat with him we are on our way towards fulfillment, we look to the end of things with joy in our hearts. St. Ignatius of Antioch calls the Eucharist "a medicine of immortality." This is an echo of our

Lord's own words: "He who eats my flesh and drinks my blood has eternal life and I will raise him up on the last day" (Jn 6:54). And so, even now we work at the healing of Christ's body, bringing relief to suffering and poverty, working toward the recovery of community and the elimination of racism and all the forces of disunity among men.

The Eucharistic sacrament must not be disconnected from our human life. When we enter a Church to worship we are not trying to escape the world but preparing ourselves to face it. Symbolically at the offertory we are putting everything on the altar table. As we take bread and wine into our hands as Christ did, we give thanks as he did for the world of creation, for the gifts of God, and we pray that he would turn these simple ordinary things into vehicles of his grace and make them bearers of his redeeming, saving power.

In his Supper Christ discloses what creation is and what it is for. The material order is God's creation; it is the sphere where we do our living, where Christ did his thing. Christ's blessing changes bread and wine, the stuff of life, into a new creation, consecrated for a holy use. The reception of the consecrated bread and wine demands that we should live consecrated lives; that we should present our "bodies as a living sacrifice holy and acceptable to God which is our spiritual worship" (Rm 12:1). Our daily life can thus become a challenge and even a joyful adventure, a celebration instead of a drudge. The more we give of ourselves in the act of receiving Christ, the more of him we will bear in our daily life; in him nature and grace, the world and its Lord become one.

Twenty

FOR THE LIFE OF THE WORLD

There are many ways in which the Eucharist is or was not a public action but a private one. In the time of persecution, not only in the first centuries but in later parallel epochs, when mere participation in a Eucharistic assembly was considered a criminal activity, secrecy was a necessary precaution in the celebration of the Eucharist. Later in the period which followed the peace of the Church, according to the principle that "the holy things are for holy people," a discipline of secrecy again prevailed when even the catechumens were not allowed to witness the principal parts of the Mass. The very nature of the Eucharist imposes limits and barriers. The Eucharistic meal is restricted to the baptized members of the body of Christ, and they alone can share in the divine life made available by our risen Lord in his Paschal mystery, the mystery of his death and resurrection. One is reminded of Peter's *prima facie* surprising statement about our Lord's resurrection: "God raised him to life and allowed him to be seen, not by the whole people but only by certain witnesses God had chosen beforehand" (Ac 10:40f). Bright light is blinding to the eye; revelation and faith mutually intertwine. To give means also to receive, and receptivity supposes compatibility and the possibility of assimilation. Yet, all in all, where all is said and done, the Eucharistic meal is essentially open to everyone and surely meant for the life of the whole world: "This is my flesh that I give for the life of the world" (Jn 5:51).

The Eucharist is the true body and blood of our Lord Jesus Christ for us Christians to eat and drink. That the reality of eating and drinking here is essentially spiritual and symbolic, should be evident from the jejune nature of the ritual meal. The communicant normally receives just about 140 milligrams (1/200 of an ounce) of unleavened bread with 3/10 of one calorie of food value. The only growth intended by this food is what St. Thomas Aquinas, with some humor, calls "*spiritus pinquedinem*" in the invitatory for the feast of Corpus Christi: "Come let us adore Christ the king, the Lord of all nations, who gives us as we feed on his body and blood a well rounded out spirit (fatness of soul)."

The Incarnation, the assumption of a human nature into the Godhead, is the very heart of salvation history, of God's plan for our salvation. And it is the Incarnate Word of God with the body-and-blood humanity which he assumed, who is present and active in the Eucharist. The Incarnated body of Christ became the crucified, dead, and risen body; the risen body is also the Eucharistic body which builds up Christ's mystical body, the Church, "until we become the perfect man fully mature with the fullness of Christ himself" (Ep 4:13), the total Christ, the whole body (1 Cor 12:12). "If we live by the truth and in love, we shall grow in all ways into Christ, who is the head by whom the whole body is fitted and joined together" (Ep 4:15f).

This is the incarnational approach to the Paschal mystery which can also be expressed in cultic, sacramental terms. The Eucharist is the most blessed of all the Sacraments, the focal center of man's cultic approach to God because Christ himself is the sacrament of our encounter with God, an effective sign or means of approaching God in total consecration and dedication. The Church by its very definition is the sacrament of Christ; etymologically and really the Church is "what is the Lord's" (*kyriake*), hence the Pauline lyricism about the glorious Spouse which Jesus takes to himself "with no speck or wrinkle or anything like that, but holy and faultless" (Ep 5:25). Finally, the Christian should be a sacrament both of the Church, a healthy member of the body of Christ (1 Cor 12:12) and a sacrament of Christ himself: "I live now not with my own life but with the life of Christ who lives in me" (Gal 2:20).

In assuming our common humanity, the Word of God united himself with all of humankind, so that there are no human limits to the identification of the Christ of the Eucharist with the one world of human beings. By his human nature, he is linked inseparably with anything human, with every person, without reference to any person's intelligence, health, sophistication, learning, experience, age, race, color, culture, or epoch. Whatever it was that made the first *homo sapiens* a human being, whatever it is that makes any of us a human being, that Christ assumed and in that humanity he is present in the holy Eucharist but as the new Adam (1 Cor 15:45), the prototype of the new humanity which God recreates in him (2 Cor 5:17) in "the goodness and holiness of the truth" (Ep 4:24).

Christ bodily, and if you will, bloodily present in the Eucharist is not merely a human being. He is *the* human being, the model, the standard, the blueprint, the die that determines what authentic humanity is, from the first human being to the last. He stands both as the initial and as the ultimate man, the exemplar of human virtue in its most eminent perfection and the one whose irrefragable integrity stands as the judgment upon all our lapses from genuine humanity. Not the least of his virtues is the unselfishness which he exhibits in the act which the Eucharist primarily makes present again, his sacrificial death on the cross for our benefit, the climax and epitome of his redemptive work, of his unswerving obedience to his heavenly Father. And this sacrifice which is made present before God and before the Eucharistic assembly is a sacrifice for the whole world. It celebrates the victory of Christ, a victory which he and God accomplished in him both in his death and resurrection. He is the true Lamb of God who has taken away the sins of the world (Jn 1:29) and by rising to life again restored to the world of human beings everlasting life (Rv 1:18). In the Eucharist all of God's act in Christ is made present before God and before us: his birth, his perfect life of obedience, his last supper, his passion, death and resurrection, and, in anticipation, his glorious coming at the Parousia. All this was offered to God for the whole world. It is retroactive to the first human being, and it thrusts forward in its saving effect to the end of time. The one and only sacrifice of Christ (Heb 7:27) is the center of salvation history; Christ is the one priest and the one victim offered for all of us and for our salvation. He offers us also in him as members of his body, the Church. "The aim (of the sacrifice offered in the Eucharist) is that the entire commonwealth of the redeemed, that is, the community and the society of saints, be offered as a universal sacrifice to God through the High Priest who in his passion offered his very self for us that we might be the body of so exalted a head" (*Decree on the Ministry of Priests*, no. 2).

The Christ who gives his body and blood in the Eucharist and makes us all one body with him and with all his holy Church through the one loaf and the one cup (1 Cor 10:17) is the one through whom all things were made, for whom all were made, and in whom all things hang together (Col 1:14-17). The Word of God, the true light which enlightens every man (Jn 1:9), who became man in order that human beings might be partakers of the divine nature (2 P 1:4), is the focal point of creation. Through him the Father made all things, the universe, space and time, and everything which fills them, with the world of human beings as the summit and climax of creation (Ps 8:5f). Without him was not anything made (Jn 1:1, 3, 10). And the Father did not only make everything *through* his Son, but also *in* him and *for* him. "The Son of God in whom we have redemption, the forgiveness of sins, is the image of the invisible God, the firstborn of all creation, for in him all things were created in heaven and on earth, visible and invisible, all things were created through him and for him, so that he is the goal toward which creation is moving. He is before all things and in him all things hold together" (Col 1:14-1). Especially in our day we need to be able to affirm that our whole universe hangs together in Christ. We need the assurance that our world is not a gigantic accident but that it is our Father's world, which he made through and for his Son. The Lord Jesus sitting, not only as God but also as man, at God's right hand holds the world together making ultimate sense of its terrifying absurdities.

Because we eat the body and drink the blood of this cosmic Christ, we are bound in him to his concerns. As we share the Eucharistic bread with Christ each of us must, according to our vocation, influence, and resources, seek to redeem the area of our own influence for Christ. Because he is preeminently the man who is the model of all men, nothing human is alien to him. In his lifetime he manifested himself as the sworn enemy of injustice, disease, prejudice, discrimination, and exploitation, and he is calling us to an imitation of himself in these areas also. Like him we must show reverence for his gifts of creation, concern for minorities, the outcasts, publicans and sinners (Lk 15:1).

The Eucharist is a symbol of the renewal of all things by Christ and in Christ. This appears even in the material elements of the sacrament. The bread and wine are easily seen not only as the work of God's creation but also as the work of human hands and the result of human skills and knowledge. Thus the bread and wine stand as it were as symbols of the whole sweep of human activity. Our Lord takes this God-given and man-made bread and wine and by his mighty word makes it his body and blood. In so doing he affirms his right by creation and conquest to all the creatures of God's hand, to all the fruits of human labor, and to all the orders and institutions of the universe.

The Eucharist is also the occasion for the Church's intercessions on behalf of all the world. It is at the Eucharist that historically the Church has offered her most fervent "supplications, prayers, intercessions, and thanksgivings for all men, for kings and for all who are in high positions, that we may lead a quiet and peaceful life, godly and respectful in every way" (1 Tm 2:1-2). This is evident from the text of the liturgy, throughout the ages.

Finally, the Eucharist is part of our preparation for service to the whole world. The Holy Eucharist is not the only channel of the Holy Spirit, but it is a unique one from which we cannot dispense ourselves. According to Patristic tradition it is by eating our Lord's body and drinking his blood that we have the divine remedy against sin, flesh, devil, world, death, danger, and hell, and a bestowing of grace, life, paradise, Christ, and God. In holy Communion we have a safeguard against death, a food of the soul, a refreshment of our faith in the battle of life, a consolation of over-burdened hearts, a treasure from heaven, a precious antidote against the poison of weakness, and a pure, wholesome, soothing medicine which aids and quickens us in both soul and body. It is especially by our participation in this sacrament that we can become effective agents of Christ in our own individual universes of influence. It is not an accident that Eucharistic renewal and a renewal of the Church's awareness of her servant role outside the walls of her buildings have always tended to go hand in hand, and that real liturgy and a sense of awareness of the Christian responsibility for society are mutually interdependent, like the love of God and the love of neighbor (Mt 22:37-40).

The fellowship and the community which the Eucharist creates is universal. There is no race outside of it, just as there is no racial difference within it. There is no language in which the words of institution cannot be spoken. There is no ideology that has not had to yield to Christ in its total demand upon persons whom this sacrament has nourished. There are no divisions that it cannot transcend, no walls or curtains, iron or bamboo, that remain impenetrable to Eucharistic influence. The Eucharist can make us one body in Christ in spite of our dividedness and separations. Its thrust toward unity is more powerful than the divisive elements that fragment our world and our lives. The God who is one is finally stronger than the demons who are legion.

Our own task should be clear. We need to communicate the good news of God's act in Christ to those whom it affects, that is, to all men. It is our task in humility, in holy reverence for his world, in the kind of love for our fellow human beings which echoes the love with which he loved us, to take seriously what Christ is, what he has done, what he does, what he will do, and what he gives us when he lets us eat his body and drink his blood and makes us thereby one with him and with one another.

Twenty-one

THE REAL PRESENCE

Our human history is essentially the story of God's ever closer presence to his creatures, first in the Old Testament dispensation of promise, then by the fulfillment realized in Christ's Incarnation and Redemption. God's relations with man can be summed up as God's gift of himself to us, culminating in the mystery of the redemptive Incarnation.

Already in the Old Testament, God revealed himself as a living person, as our creator and savior, manifesting himself to men's minds but much more to their hearts, inviting all to receive him in active love. In the fullness of time, Christ's essential message was the gift of himself, the substantial, living Word, the Word made flesh, God made man. In Jesus we have divine truth showing the way leading to eternal life (Jn 14:6). Christ blazes the trail for us, leading us to that love-truth which is God himself. He treads for us the path of renunciation, of trust, and of obedience which leads to God. He makes possible our encounter with God by faith which should normally result in total commitment to God's salvific purposes.

During the whole course of salvation history God was always present to his people, manifesting himself "in many wonderful ways" first in the Old Testament theophanies and in his permanent presence in the Jewish temple, and ultimately in Christ Jesus, who assumed our human nature. God's presence to man could never be more intimate and beneficial than by the redemptive Incarnation which is clearly the climax and focal point of all God's revelation.

What the Incarnated Lord Jesus taught us and especially what he did for us remains for all times man's official and in fact the only essential way to God. Imitation and following of Christ now becomes our only approach to God, and it is all the easier because of Christ's closeness and presence to his Church and all the faithful. Jesus returned to his Father but still remains with us (Mt 28:20) in all sorts of ways until his redemptive work is fully accomplished. He lives on in his Church especially in the Liturgy, the Church's official repetition and assimilation of what Jesus said and did for our salvation.

The Last Supper and Calvary were not only the historical end of our Lord's life here below, but also its climactic consummation (Jn 19:30). The Church will now live in expectation of her Master's glorious return for the inauguration of God's eternal kingdom. All the while, faithful to our Lord's command and under the direction of his Paraclete, she remembers efficaciously the mystery of our redemption by repeating it for our assimilation and applying it to our needs. This is the burden of all the Church's liturgy of the Eucharist which is clearly the center and soul of the life of the Church here below. The Eucharist, in fact, is the treasure of the Church, the summit of its liturgy, the living source of all the sacraments and of all the activities of the Church.

Christ remains so closely united to all the work of his Church that the Church can be graphically described as his Mystical Body, because of his spiritual union with the faithful. Yet wonderful and real as it is, this spiritual presence springs from the substantial presence of Christ in the Eucharist which is the center of the whole Christian economy. The Eucharist is the sacrament of sacraments, the essential, life-giving element of the Church's liturgy, and in particular the special feature of the Holy Sacrifice of the Mass. Without Christ's real presence the Eucharistic action would be an empty symbolic shell.

There are many ways in which Christ is present to his Church accomplishing the great work of our salvation, but the heart of it all is his substantial and permanent presence under the Eucharistic species.

Christ has promised to be present to his Church when she prays (Mt 18:20) for, as St. Augustine puts it, he it is who prays for us and in us, while he is also as God attentive to our every prayer.

He is present when the Church performs her works of mercy, not only because anything we do for one of his brothers, however humble, we do for him (Mt 25-40) but also because he himself performs these works through his Church, who without him is helpless (Jn 15:15).

By grace he is present to those who believe in him for through faith he dwells in our hearts in love (Ep 3:17) and floods our inmost being through the Holy Spirit he has given us (Rm 5:5).

In another very real manner Christ is present to his preaching Church, since the Gospel which is proclaimed is God's word and is preached in Christ's name, and by his authority as God's Incarnate Word and with his assistance. In this way there is formed, according to St. Augustine, one flock safe and sound, by the action of its one shepherd. This is true especially at Mass during the official liturgy of the Word, which is a proclamation of God's wonderful works in the history of salvation, to make the mystery of Christ ever present and active within us.

Christ is present in his Church in the government of the people of God. The Church's sacred power derives from Christ, "the Shepherd of shepherds," according to St. Augustine's wonderful phrase. In a solemn promise to his Apostles (Mt 28:20) Christ guaranteed to be present to his pastors in the exercise of their pastoral duties.

In a manner still more sublime Christ is present in his Church as she offers the sacrifice of the Mass and in the administration of the sacraments.

St. John Chrysostom has an eloquent description of Christ's presence in the offering of the sacrifice of the Mass. In his view, no matter who offers it, be it Peter, or Paul, or any priest at the altar, the sacrifice is always the same which Christ gave to his disciples. Today's offering is in no way inferior since it is sanctified by Christ himself. The priest speaks the very words of Christ and in his name, and so there is always only one and the same offering. As Trent states, at Mass Christ offers, through the ministry of his priests, the same oblation of himself which he made on the Cross.

Finally, the sacraments are the actions of Christ who administers them through men. That is how and why the sacraments are holy, pouring grace into souls by the power of Christ.

Wonderful as are all these presences of Christ in his Church, there is still one that surpasses them all. It is his presence in the sacrament of the Eucharist, among all the other instruments of grace, the most consoling source of devotion, the most satisfying object of contemplation, and the most effective means of sanctification. How could it be otherwise since this blessed Sacrament contains Christ himself and is thus the summit of the spiritual life and the perfection of all the sacraments?

The presence of Christ is called real par excellence and pre-eminently. The other presences of Christ are real also but here we have presence in the fullest ontological sense, a substantial presence by which Christ, the God-man, is wholly and entirely present, truly, really, and substantially as the Council of Trent specified.

In the Eucharist Christ is present with the totality of his being: body, blood, soul, and divinity, truly, really, and substantially present. Truly since his words "this is my body" must be understood in their literal proper meaning. Such was clearly the faith of the primitive Church, which rests ultimately on the interpretation that our Lord himself gave to his own words (Jn 6). Christ is really present and not merely in a symbolic way as expressed in several other Biblical assertions (e.g., Jn 15:1; 1 Cor 10:4). Substantially also for it is the very being of Christ, human and divine, that becomes present, and not merely his divine power of sanctification as in the other sacraments or presences described above.

Christ's salvific mission consisted essentially in the *gift of himself*, of all that he is in his full and total reality, human and divine, to his Father and to his Church. This he did officially at the Last Supper and on Calvary. He loved as far as love could go, giving himself inseparably to his Father and to the Church; to his Father on Calvary for the Church, and to the Church in the Cenacle for his Father's glory.

The reality of the gift on Calvary called for the full reality of the Eucharistic gift. The act of redemption was the total gift of divine love in our behalf, as well as the absolute homage rendered to God in our name. The Eucharist could have been an empty remembrance of this supreme gift. Actually, it is God's renewed gift of his Son, as well as Christ's gift of himself to his Father in the name of all humanity, but especially of his Mystical Body.

Christ is present in the Eucharist as our food and drink but first and above all as our Priest and victim. The Mass is the sacramental actualization, the existential, concrete application of Christ's unique sacrifice. It is first of all the supreme homage of adoration to God, but also the highest possible glorification of the Incarnate Word. It manifests the love which led Christ to his death and Resurrection, continues his nuptial banquet with the Church, and preludes the eternal nuptials of the Lamb with the new Jerusalem (Rv 19-21).

Christ in the Eucharist is Priest and victim of our sacrifice and the host of our communion; such is the essential purpose of the institution of this sacrament and it remains true as long as the sacrament endures. The Eucharistic bread has clearly no other possible origin than the Mass or ultimate destination but holy communion. However, because of the very nature of the sacrament which includes Christ's presence, the Church has drawn some practical conclusions and specific practices: for example, the reserve of the sacrament for the sick; or the so-called fermentum or fragments sent from the Papal Mass to the parish churches to typify the unity of the faith; and especially reverence for the presence of Christ in the sacrament.

Veneration and respect for the sacrament must be as ancient in the Church as the institution itself of the Eucharist. That seems to be a sure conclusion from St. Paul's famous admonition to the Corinthians (1 Cor 11:28-32). And from the earliest liturgies even to our own holy Mass, it seems clear that the proper veneration for the Blessed Sacrament is adoration.

It is not surprising then that with time and under the influence of certain historical tendencies and needs, such as devotion to the sacred humanity of Christ, and the Protestant denials of the Real Presence, specific adoration of Christ present in the Eucharist was developed and sanctioned by the Church.

Exposition of the Blessed Sacrament and Eucharistic devotions as practiced in our day are in the line of unessential religious phenomena, but have their own convenience and utility. Far from obscuring the essential Eucharistic mystery of Mass and Communion, they actually spring from the Liturgy and prepare for a richer liturgical participation.

Such at least was the mind of St. Peter Julian Eymard who proposed the method of the four ends of the sacrifice of the Mass, adoration, thanksgiving, reparation, and prayer, as the ideal, the perfect exemplar for meditative prayer before the Blessed Sacrament exposed. The Saint also suggested that adoration of the Blessed Sacrament should be made under the influence of the grace of Holy Communion. It would then be a type of spiritual communion, an act of union with our Lord.

Christ exposed in the holy Eucharist receives our homage and is active in the dialogue which is essential in meditative prayer. His presence is an invitation to the holy union to which the sacrament is ordained, and a perpetual reminder of the holy sacrifice from which it originated. The exposition is also a fine reminder of Christ's eternal priesthood (Heb 7:23-25) which finds in the Mass its temporal exercise.

Twenty-two

PRAYER AND WORSHIP

Prayer is a dialogue between man and God, a situation which supposes that the two have met and know each other. It is God who first manifests himself to man, in answer to the need for the infinite which each human being carries in himself. As St. Augustine puts it: "God made us for himself and nothing else but God can really satisfy our craving for happiness."

Prayer is essential to the religious man, as thinking is essential to a being endowed with intelligence; and man has no intelligent choice but to be religious. The religious man is the one who, because of a direct or indirect experience, sees in the divinity a power or a being acting with superhuman energy in the world. This experience creates a need for communication which man has always felt, at all levels of human culture. The basic aspiration to fulfill in the best way possible his own existence is part of this need. Left to his own devices, or even with the help of the society in which he lives, man cannot realize all his potential, or free himself from a sense of solitude and even of futility because of the inevitable nature of death. By himself a man cannot bring his ideal into existence. By his contact with the divinity, source of blessing, man seeks to obtain what he lacks in the normal framework of his existence, and opens himself to a superior sphere which alone can effect the full development of his potentialities.

The dialogue of prayer is the means of communication, the bridge by which the limited creature reaches the creator, the master with unlimited power. There is no religion without prayer. Prayer is the clearest expression of a living religion, more than rites, dogmas or theological systems. And being a dialogue, prayer supposes contact with the divinity; it demands mutual relations and reciprocal exchange. It is in the experience of the one who prays that this contact is made. And the divinity is constantly available through revelation which is concretized in the revealed word of God which is the Bible.

There is an essential relation between prayer and revelation. We pray our faith and prayer develops our faith. Prayer cannot be simply relegated to the ascetic life, as if it were not the purest expression of faith. Prayer is a source of revelation, not only negatively in the sense that traditional prayer is a safeguard of our faith, but also positively. Prayer matures our faith, and the biblical prayers throughout the centuries are an important, positive source to understand God's progressive self-revelation. Prayer is inseparable from the religious history of God's chosen people and the spiritual message of God's revelation contained in the Bible.

Man's essential duty to God can be stated in one word, worship, which is reverence and service of God. Now prayer is one of the essential elements of worship, another being sacrifice which is external worship. Prayer is of its very nature worship.

When cultic acts lack religious value because they are without corresponding interior dispositions, it is prayer under the form of a supplication or a song which fulfills their role. "You who wanted no sacrifice or oblation opened my ear, you asked no holocaust or sacrifice for sin; then I said, here I am, I am coming. Am I not commanded to do your will" (Ps 40:6-7)? Obedience is better than sacrifice (1 S 15:22). This emphasis should be interpreted in the light of similar prophetic statements on sacrifice. It singles out dedication and commitment as the only adequate response to God, without, of course, rejecting the principle of sacrifice.

The prophets (Am 5:21) often attack religious hypocrisy, the conviction that all is well, provided external forms, like sacrifice and fasting, are observed though the most elementary principles of social justice and brotherly love are neglected. The Psalmists also emphasize the prayerful attitude, the inner dispositions which must lie behind acceptable sacrifice, namely, obedience, gratitude, contrition. The book of Chronicles, too, insists on the part played in sacrificial worship by the liturgical chant as an expression of inward sentiments. All these authors protest against a religion of mere form. The New Testament will take up the theme (Lk 11:41-42; Mt 7:21) and inculcate "worship in spirit and in truth" (Jn 4:21-24). The Holy Spirit who makes a new creature of man (Jn 3:5) is also the inspiring principle of the new worship.

The sacrifice acceptable to God is a broken spirit; "a broken and contrite heart, O God, you will not despise" (Ps 51-17). A contrite heart is one in which sorrow and affliction have done their work, and the obstinacy of pride has been replaced by the humility of penitence. Spiritual sacrifices of praise and thanksgiving are more acceptable than the most perfect animal victim (Ps 69:31). "My prayers rise like incense, my hands like the evening offering" (Ps 141:2). Prayer here is the equivalent of sacrifice, showing how closely Jewish piety associated prayer with sacrifice.

Prayer accompanies the act of worship as an integral part. The ancient traditions show that when an altar was erected or a sacrifice offered, the name of the divinity was invoked (Gn 12:8, 13:4, 26:25, 1 K 18:32). "Abraham built an altar to Yahweh (between Bethel and Ai) and invoked the name of Yahweh" (Gn 12:8). The expression, "call by means of the name," denotes the essential act in worship, the invocation, or rather evocation, of the deity by the solemn utterance of his name. It rests on the widespread primitive idea that a real bond exists between the person and his name. In the New Testament, Christians style themselves as those who invoke the name of the Lord (Ac 9:14, 21); the title Lord no longer indicates Yahweh but Jesus (Ph 2:11). By invoking the name of Jesus his power is stirred to action (Ac 3:6). Faith, of course, is required if this invocation is to be effective. The name for whose sake the apostles suffer (Ac 21:13), the name they preach (4:10, 12) and which Christians invoke (2:21) is the name, that is, the person of Jesus (3:16), the name he received at his resurrection (2:36), the name above all other names. This name was Lord, hitherto reserved to God (Ph 2:9-11). The proclamation "Jesus is Lord" (Rm 10:9; 1 Cor 12:3) is the essence of the Christian Creed and worship.

The ritual legislation of Leviticus and Deuteronomy seldom alludes to prayer, yet has preserved some formulas of liturgical prayer. Dt 26:5-10 presents a cultic credo, a profession of faith which reminds Israel of the divine choice (5), of deliverance from Egypt (6-8), and of the gift of the promised land (9). This is an ancient creedal recital of the Lord's mighty acts, a sort of Israelite Apostles' Creed because it summarizes Israel's sacred history. Dt 26:12-15 contains a liturgy for the ceremony of the triennial tithing. It is a solemn profession of obedience in the past (12-14) with a prayer for a blessing in the future (15).

The cultic acts of mourning, penance, fasting, lamentation, confession are all accompanied with prayer (1 S 7:6;2 K 19:1; 2 M 8:29). An especially good example is found in Ezr 9:5-15, a passage known as Ezra's confession. This prayer, which is also a sermon, contains a genuine confession of sin.

The interest which Joel displays in formal observance and the liturgy (1:9, 13, 16, 2:14) contrasts markedly with the attitude of Amos; but he also insists on the need for inward conversion. "Let your hearts be broken, not your garments" (2:13).

There are in the Old Testament a succession of great prayer-hymns which are as it were the backbone of biblical revelation. The first and most famous of these canticles which the Christian liturgy takes from the Old Testament is Moses' song of victory (Ex 15:1-21). A victory chant (1, 21) becomes a whole psalm of thanksgiving; its starting point is the destruction of Pharoah's army (4-5) but it goes on to develop the theme of God's power and his care for his people (6-9); the wonders of the Exodus (10-13), the conquest of Canaan (14-16), even the building of the temple in Jerusalem (17-18).

The Song of Deborah and Barak (Jg 5:1-31), a masterpiece of ancient Hebrew literature, notwithstanding its savagery (24-27), is instinct with genuine love for the God of Israel. "Let those who love you be like the sun as he arises in all his might" (31). The song is built around a complex standard pattern consisting of the woven theological motifs of Yahweh's glory, the Sinai experience, the conquest of Canaan, and the worship of Yahweh.

These themes are constantly repeated in the biblical hymns; they are the elements of the basic memorial theme of remembering effectively the mighty works of God. This anamnesis is essential not only in salvation history but also in its liturgical counterpart, the temple worship (Ps 136) and the Christian Eucharistic celebration: "Do this as a memorial of me" (1 Cor 11:24).

The book of Tobit concludes with a hymn of praise (ch. 13), an echo of Old Testament passages. The first part (1-8) is a song of thanksgiving; the second (9-17) addresses Jerusalem in the style of the prophets, expressing the exiles' hope for an ideal Jerusalem.

In the book of Judith a similar poem (ch. 16) occupies a similar position at the end of the book. It summarizes the whole story in typical Hebrew poetry. The finale repeats a well-known theme: "A little thing indeed is a sweetly smelling sacrifice, still less the fat burned for you in holocaust; but whoever fears the Lord is great forever" (16:16). It was the custom of biblical editors to insert poems into their work to increase artistic and especially religious appeal by introducing the transcendent view into human history. In 1 Samuel (2) we find the Song of Hannah whose greatest claim to fame is perhaps the fact that it became the model for Mary's Magnificat (Lk 1:46-55). The poem opens with a jubilant profession of faith in God, the outcome presumably of some signal display of divine mercy (1-2). The author then rebukes his enemies for their arrogant attitude towards Yahweh (3). The central thought, Yahweh's government of the world, is developed in a series of antithetic clauses illustrating his control over the destinies of mankind (4-8). God's dominion is a guarantee that he will preserve his holy ones and destroy the wicked (9). Finally, the coming judgment will result in the exaltation of God's anointed one, the Messiah (19).

Jonah's prayer (2:2-9) is a mosaic of psalm texts constructed on the conventional pattern of thanksgiving psalms: description of sufferings undergone, account of deliverance from them (2-6), an acknowledgement of Yahweh as deliverer, a religious lesson, and an announcement of a temple offering (7-9). The analogy between Christian baptism and the resurrection of Christ has led to the use of the figure of Jonah in baptismal typology (Mt 12:40, Rom 6:4).

Habakkuk also closes with a long prayer (ch. 3) which combines supplication with a hymn to the omnipotence of God, extolling the marching forth of the Lord in victory for the salvation of his people. The poet contemplates God's power and asks for his mercy (2); he pictures God's coming in majesty (3-4) and the terrible effect upon nature (5-11), the punishment of the wicked (12-14) and his final triumph (15). Finally, the prophet expresses his fear (16-17) but immediately also his trust in God's mercy (18-19).

One of the two appendices found at the end of Ecclesiasticus (51:1-12) is a psalm of thanksgiving for deliverance. The author sees in his own experience of distress and rescue not something purely personal but a demonstration in part of Yahweh's merciful dealings with the people as a whole.

Finally, 2 Maccabees (1:23-29) offers a fine example of the closeness of sacrifice and prayer. "And while the sacrifice was being consumed, the priests offered prayer, the priest and everyone. Jonathan led and the rest responded, as did Nehemiah. The prayer was to this effect: O Lord, Lord God, creator of all things, dreadful, strong, just, almighty and everlasting, the only king and benefactor, the only provider, who alone are just, almighty and everlasting, the deliverer of Israel from every evil, who made our fathers your chosen ones and sanctified them, accept this sacrifice in behalf of all your people Israel, and protect your heritage and consecrate it. Bring together all who are dispersed, set free those in slavery among the heathen, look favorably on those held in contempt or abhorrence, and let the heathen know that you are our God. Punish those who oppress us and affront us by their insolence, and plant your people firmly in your Holy Place, as Moses promised."

Twenty-three

PRAYER OF ADORATION

The prayer of praise contemplates God's transcendence, his immensity and beauty; it sings his attributes, his works to exalt him and adore. Adoration is the actual act of homage and worship; it gives glory to God which according to St. Augustine's fine description is "clear knowledge of God accompanied by praise." It supposes that God has revealed himself in religious experiences which allow man to measure his power and his providence. Praise is man's reaction, his answer. It constitutes the highest form of prayer, comparable to that addressed to God most high by the heavenly spirits: "Holy, Holy, Holy is Yahweh Sabaoth. His glory fills the whole earth" (Is 6:3). This trisagion has deservedly had a great influence on Jewish and Christian liturgy (Rv 4:8).

Acclamation is one of the simplest and most spontaneous forms of the prayer of praise. Nb 10:5 mentions the sacred battle cry; it was a fierce shout for encouraging the fighters and throwing the enemy into panic. In Jos 6:5, 20 the whole people utter a mighty war cry and the walls of Jericho collapse then and there. The blast of the trumpet and the loud shout are the ancient rites of holy war (Jg 7:20). This was also part of the ark ritual (1 S 4:5). Each stage of the journey in the wilderness is regarded as a march to battle. Trumpets and acclamations were also used at religious festivals (Lv 25:1); there was even a feast of Acclamations (Nb 29:1-6). Originally a battle cry, the acclamations had strong religious overtones and were later incorporated into the temple liturgy and certain psalms. The feast of Acclamations was celebrated on the first day of the seventh month (Tishri) (Nb 29:1) and was probably meant to keep alive the memory of the pre-exilic beginning of both the religious year and the civil year in the autumn. In the religious calendar of Lv 23 and Nb 28-29, the religious year began with the feast of Passover in the spring. Judaism in New Testament times (and today) celebrated the civil feast of New Year (Rosh Hashana) at the beginning of the month of Tishri.

A *proclamation* of faith in God can also be a part of the prayer of praise. When all the people saw Elijah's sacrifice "they fell on their faces. Yahweh is God, they cried, Yahweh is God!" (1 K 18:39). In 2 K 5:15 Naaman says: "Now I know that there is no God in all the earth except in Israel." And king Nebuchadnezzar says to Daniel: "Your God must be the God of gods, the master of kings, and the Revealer of mysteries, since you have been able to reveal this mystery" (Dn 2:47).

The eulogy or *blessing* constitutes another well defined type of praise; it is found from the very beginning and is used at all times. It is a benediction expressing a desire for happiness, or extolling the virtues or services of someone. Man's blessing of another man is a supplication addressed to God, asking him for all sorts of benefits (Gn 28:3, 49:28). The essence of God's blessing of man is the placing of the divine name on the people (Nb 6:27). The name was used in antiquity for the person. The actual placing of the divine name on Israel not only declares that they belong to God but also ensures prosperity. The simplest and fullest expression of divine blessing is found in the promise of God in Gn 26:3: "I will be with you." Hence the high prayer value of our frequent liturgical greeting: "The Lord be with you." In Ruth 2:4 we find Boaz saying to his reapers: "Yahweh be with you," and they reply: "Yahweh bless you."

When God is blessed, the blessing is equivalent to praise, since it is the proclamation of some divine attribute. The formulas begin with: "Blessed be God who". . . and there follows a description of the divine works, and a recall of divine attributes, all of which provoke praise. Melchizedek "pronounced this blessing: Blessed be Abram by God, Most High, creator of heaven and earth, and blessed be God Most High for handing over your enemies to you" (Gn 14:20). In ancient narratives the formulas are very brief.

This is man's reaction in an attitude of thanksgiving before a divine favor. The formula is later developed and becomes a mode of expression for praise and adoration. "Blessed be God! Blessed be his great name! Blessed be all his holy angels! Blessed be his great name forevermore! For he has scourged me and now has pity on me and I see my son Tobias" (Tb 11:14-15). Blessing God is a constant refrain in the Psalter. "I will bless Yahweh at all times, his praise shall ever be on my lips" (Ps 34:1). "Yahweh, all your creatures thank you, and your faithful bless you" (145:10).

Ps 116:12-13 deserves special attention. "What return can I make to Yahweh for all his goodness to me? I will offer libations to my savior, invoking the name of Yahweh." The cup of salvation is a reference to a liturgical thanksgiving ritual: the saving cup, the cup offered to God who saves. In 1 Cor 10:16 the Eucharist is characterized as "the cup of blessing," the cup of wine for which we thank God as Christ did at the Last Supper. We bless the cup, that is, pronounce a blessing over it, invoke God's blessing over it in imitation of our Lord at the Last Supper; and God makes our blessing operative: the cup of blessing is also a blessed cup, a source of blessing for us.

The first four books of the Psalter each end with a praise formula in the form of a eulogy. "Blessed be Yahweh, the God of Israel from eternity and forever! Amen, Amen!"(41:13)."Blessed be Yahweh, the God of Israel who alone performs these marvels! Blessed forever be his glorious name, may the whole world be filled with his glory! Amen, Amen!" (72:18-19). "Blessed be Yahweh forever! Amen, Amen!" (89-51). "Blessed be Yahweh, the God of Israel, from all eternity and forever! Here all the people are to say, Amen!" (106:48). A more elaborate doxology concludes the whole Psalter at the end of book five (Ps 150). It invites every musical instrument, the full orchestra, and every living being to praise the Lord, Yahweh (cf. Rv 5:13).

In 2 Ch 20:26 is an interesting example of etiology, the assignment of an explanation, a cause or a reason, to some place or event. "On the fourth day they mustered in the valley of Beracah (blessing) and there they did indeed bless Yahweh, hence the name of the valley of Beracah by which the place is still called today."

Corresponding to the blessing of God is the *beatitude* (macharism), the happiness of man. A beatitude is a declaration of blessedness on the ground of some virtue or gift of God. It is associated with prayer and wisdom utterances. It is a sapiential form common especially in the Psalms. In fact, it is characteristically the opening word of the Psalter (Ps 1:1). Literally, "Oh! the blessednesses," an exclamation of felicitation found at the beginning of some other psalms. The plural indicates that the person described enjoys all the true joys and that nothing is lacking to his happiness.

One is called blessed for virtue or for enjoying the forgiveness, protection, or nearness of God. Beatitudes are common in the New Testament also, most frequently for faith (Jn 20:29) or for sharing the kingdom of God. Best known are the beatitudes uttered by Jesus (Mt 5:3-5). Revelation (1:3 etc.) has seven beatitudes, a favorite biblical theme of promise and consolation.

It is the *hymn* which remains the normal expression of praise and adoration. By its poetic form it places art at the service of religious experience, as a mode of expression. Judging by their insertion in the course of the historical narratives, hymns originated as a joyful reaction to a victory (Jg 5) or a wonderful manifestation of God (2 S 22). Sacred history perpetuated the souvenir of these liberating experiences which are also recalled in the feasts by the successive generations. The religious poet expresses his own interior experience, his intimate reactions to the manifestations of God recalled by tradition and celebrated in the feasts. The hymn gives history its religious dimension by making it the theater of an active presence of Yahweh; it is the hagiographer's way of introducing the transcendent in salvation history.

It is by these interventions in history that God reveals his attributes, his power, his majesty, his providence. His universal supremacy makes him the protector of the Jewish nation. As history develops, the object of the hymn is enriched. To the history of the patriarchs, with the themes of election and of the promises, is added the liberation from Egypt, the sojourn in the wilderness, the conquest and the possession of the promised land; then comes the election of David and of Sion, the exile and the restoration, and finally, in the distance, the eschatological time presented by the prophets as a return to paradise, the garden of Eden, with the triumph of goodness, justice, and peace.

The hymn crystallizes the religious sentiments experienced by the people or the individual before a God who reveals himself as powerful, majestic, provident, accessible and desirable. The hymn, finally, constitutes the type itself of divine praise, when it was originally a simple spontaneous reaction to a passing event: for example, Moses' song of victory, after the crossing of the Red Sea (Ex 15:20-21). The hymn naturally found a place in the celebration of feasts, and when the official worship of praise was established, the Levitical choirs sang the hymns in the temple. "David appointed some of the Levites as ministers before the ark of Yahweh to commemorate, glorify, and praise Yahweh the God of Israel" (1 Ch 16:4).

The hymns of the Old Testament are found throughout the historical books (Tb 13; 1 Ch 29:10-19; Ezr 9:6-15; Ne 1:5-11) and the prophetic books (Hab 3), but especially in the Psalter. Many of them have a specific theme: the God of nature (Ps 8, 19, 29), the God of history (Ps 42, 105), God, the universal king (Ps 147, 148).

The hymn is the easiest type to identify; its structure, language and tone are always the same. The usual structure of the hymn includes three parts: the introduction, the body, and the conclusion. The introduction is an invitation to praise; it is addressed to living persons or to personified beings, on earth or in heaven, pressing them to celebrate the name of Yahweh, his attributes and his mighty deeds. This invitation is a rhetorical process, but is already praise. In the body of the hymn are enumerated the very reasons for praise, with an inventory of the works of God and the exaltation of his glorious attributes, especially his special providence for Israel. The conclusion is a synthesis of the general theme and a reprise of the introduction.

The hymn expresses gratitude and admiration; it translates the aspirations of the soul to God, its adoration. It is the tribute which Israel renders to Yahweh either in the promised land or in the diaspora, a tribute which hopefully all men will render as they come to know God; such is ultimately the hope of Israel. "Camels in throngs will cover you, and dromedaries of Midian and Ephah; everyone in Sheba will come, bringing gold and incense, and singing the praise of Yahweh" (Is 60:6). This is part of the description of the glorious resurrection of Jerusalem (Is 60:1-22). The riches of the sea (5), that is, the maritime powers, Phoenicia and Greece, come from the west. The riches of the East and of Egypt come by caravans across the deserts of Syria and Sinai respectively. Midian, Ephah, and Sheba are peoples of Arabia. All the peoples come to worship in Jerusalem. The liturgy applies this text to the visit of the Magi (Mt 2:1-12); the immediate significance of the text is somewhat different but its world-wide outlook makes its application apt.

The world-wide view, foreseeing a future gathering of the nations round Jerusalem to worship the God of Israel, is one of the key ideas of the Isaian book of consolation (Is 40-55). It appears also after the exile in Zechariah and Jonah; Ps 87 presents Zion as the mother of all nations. Finally, the Hebrew scribes who authored the biblical hymns, naturally come to mind as one reads about the universal appeal of the true scholar: "Nations will proclaim his wisdom, the assembly will celebrate his praise" (Si 39:10).

In the New Testament, the praise of God is a favorite Lucan theme: Luke's gospel of the Infancy contains the well-known hymns: the Magnificat (1:46-55), the Benedictus (1:67-79) and the Nunc Dimittis (2:29-32). There are several other briefer hymns, apparently early Christian credal formulas which may have had an autonomous existence in the framework of the Liturgy, before being introduced into their literary context: Ep 5:14, 1 Tm 3:14-16, 1 Tm 6:15-16, Ph 2:6-11, Col 1:15-20, 2 Tm 2:11-13, Jn 1:1-18.

Twenty-four

THE DIVINITY OF CHRIST

The New Testament clearly bears witness to the divinity of Christ. The Johannine tradition is especially evident and categorical. "The word was God" (1:1). And the doubting Thomas brings us back to this first line of John's gospel as he speaks the language which became the common Christian confession concerning Christ: "My Lord and my God" (20:28; Ac 2:36). The wheel of the gospel has come full circle; in fact, God's revelation itself reaches here its climax. Paradoxically it is the doubter who makes the most complete affirmation of Christ's nature to be found on the lips of anyone in the gospel. The combination Lord and God (*kyrios theos*) is to be found in the Septuagint to translate the name of the God of Israel (*Yahweh Elohim*); it was also a combination used as a divine designation in the Hellenistic world. The note struck in the beginning of John's gospel rings out again in its ending. And John's testimony to the life of Jesus is meant to lead men to precisely this confession of Jesus: "that you may believe that Jesus is the Christ, the Son of God, and that believing you may have life through his name" (20:31). It is interesting to note that the first gospel line to be written formulates the same faith: "the gospel about Jesus Christ, the Son of God" (Mk 1:1). These expressions of post-Pentecostal faith surely suppose a long, normal process of maturation, but this development of Christian faith creates no problem except for those who refuse to see an essential continuity between the Jesus of history and the Jesus of faith.

In the Bible the title, son of God, does not necessarily mean a natural sonship like Christ's in relation to God the Father. It may imply a sonship which is merely adoptive, that is, expressing simply a close relation to God.

The expression, son of, is common in the Bible as an adjectival substitute. Thus a son of peace (Lk 10:6) or of light (16:8) is one who loves peace and is characterized by light; the sons of thunder (Mk 3:17) are thunderbolts, and Barnabas (Ac 4:36) means son of consolation, that is, comforter. Son of man, Ezechiel's favorite expression, simply means a human being. Son of God consequently describes the result of a deliberate choice by which God sets up a very intimate relationship with some of his creatures. Thus the title is given to angels (Jb 1:6), to the chosen people (Ex 4:22), to individual Israelites (Dt 14:1; Mt 5:9, 45) and to their leaders (Ps 82:6). It is also attributed to the royal Messiah (1 Ch 17:13; Ps 2:7) but does not necessarily imply that he is more than man. The same is true when the title is used by Satan at Christ's temptation Mt 4:3, 6) or by the possessed Mk 3:11) or the centurion at the foot of the cross (Mk 15:39). Likewise, in the first context, the voice of the Father at Christ's baptism (Mt 3:17) and at the Transfiguration (17:5) suggests no more than the divine predilection for the Messiah-servant. And in all probability the high priest's question (26:63) concerns Messiahship only, but our Lord's answer (64) goes much further as everyone understood.

The title, son of God, however, can and often does bear the further, more profound meaning of sonship in the full sense of the word. Jesus clearly had this meaning in mind when he spoke of himself as the Son (Mk 21:37) ranking above the angels (Mt 24:36). These are still distant allusions but our Lord also implied more clearly that he had God for his Father in a way others had not (Mt 7:21; Jn 20:17) and that he enjoyed with the Father an altogether singular relationship of knowledge and love: "No one knows the Son except the Father, just as no one knows the Father except the Son and those to whom the Son chooses to reveal him" (Mt 11:27). This passage clearly has a Johannine flavor and has been described as a meteor from the Johannine heaven. Actually, it shows that awareness of Christ's divine sonship exists in the deepest stratum of the synoptic tradition as well as in the Johannine.

Along with Christ's assertions of his filial relationship with the Father, there are others that speak of the Messiah's divine rank (Mt 22:42-46) and of the heavenly origin of the Son of Man (8:20). This title which originally meant simply man, underlined the lowliness of man's state. But it also suggested glory because of its use in Dn 7:13 to indicate the transcendent figure, heavenly in origin, who was to receive from God's hand the eschatological kingdom, the kingdom at the end of times. In this way the title both veiled and hinted at the sort of Messiah Jesus was. Christ's explicit avowal in the presence of the Sanhedrin (Mt 26:64) should, however, have removed all ambiguity. All these assertions of Christ were finally confirmed by the triumph of his resurrection and endowed the expression, Son of God, with that strictly divine significance which it has in St. Paul: "Jesus Christ our Lord who was proclaimed Son of God in all his power through his resurrection from the dead" (Rm 1:4). For St. Paul Christ, by his resurrection, is established in glory as Lord (*Kyrios*) (Ph 2:9-11) deserving anew, this time in virtue of his Messianic work, the name he had from all eternity, Son of God.

During his lifetime, our Lord's disciples apparently had no clear idea of his divinity. But it is equally true that Jesus expressed with his own lips, gradually and with increasing clarity, his own personal consciousness of being Son of the Father in the fullest sense. On these historical utterances the faith of the disciples rested, a faith which reached its perfection after the resurrection with the help of the Holy Spirit. He is the Spirit of truth, leading men to the very fullness of truth (Jn 16:13) by leading them to understand the mystery of Christ (14:26).

Paul himself rarely gives Jesus the title God as he does in Rm 9:5: "Christ who is above all, God forever blessed! Amen"; and in Tt 2:13: "We are waiting in hope, for the blessing which will come with the Appearing of the glory of our great God and savior, Jesus Christ." Paul usually keeps the title, God, for the Father (1 Cor 8:5-6). This reflects the restraint of the early Church, which though it came to acknowledge Jesus' divinity, did not, however, quickly transfer to him the title God, no doubt as a last vestige of the Old Testament monotheism. Paul considers the divine persons not so much with an abstract appreciation of their nature as with a concrete consideration of their function in salvation history. Moreover, he has always in mind the historical Christ in his concrete reality of God made man. That is why he presents Christ as somehow subordinated to the Father: "you belong to Christ and Christ belongs to God" (1 Cor 3:23); "God is the head of Christ" (1 Cor 11:3); not only in the work of creation (1 Cor 8:6), but also in that of eschatological renewal: "The Son himself will be subject in his turn to the One who subjected all things to him so that God may be all in all" (1 Cor 15:28). The way, however, was finally paved for the Trinitarian liturgical formulas which offer the ultimately objective and demythologized divine reality.

The New Testament doxologies are apparently the expression of the original Christian cultic tradition, and the high water mark of Christian belief! Jewish literature reserved doxologies for God the Father. Paul at times betrays his Jewish background by spontaneously uttering a doxology at the climactical mention of God as the Creator, "who is blessed for ever, Amen!" (Rm 1:25, cf. Rm 11:36; 2 Cor 11:31). He has on rare occasions a doxology to Christ: "Christ who is above all, God for ever blessed! Amen" (Rm 9:5). There is also 1 Tm 3:16 where Paul is quoting an early Christian hymn; and Heb 13:21, "through Jesus Christ, to whom be glory forever and ever! Amen."

Paul addresses some doxologies to the Father and the Son together: "give glory therefore to him through Jesus Christ forever and ever. Amen" (Rm 16:27); "Glory to him whose power, working in us, can do infinitely more than we can ask or imagine; glory to him from generation to generation in the Church and in Christ Jesus forever and ever. Amen" (Ep 3:20). Finally, appears the perfect Trinitarian doxology: "the grace of the Lord Jesus Christ, the love of God, and the fellowship of the Holy Spirit be with you all" (2 Cor 13:13).

For Paul Jesus is essentially the Son of God (Rm 1:3-4, 9), *his*, that is, the Father's Son, his own Son (8:3, 32), the Son of his love (Col 1:13), his beloved Son his dear Son, a description of the unique relationship between Jesus and God. Beloved has the connotation of only-begotten monogenes (Jn 1:18), describing a quality of Jesus, his uniqueness, not what is called in Trinitarian theology his procession. Christ belongs to the sphere from which he came; "the second man is from heaven" (1 Cor 15:47) being sent by God (Rm 8:3).

The title Son of God became his in a new way with the resurrection (Rm 1:4) but it was not then that he received it since he pre-existed not only as prefigured in the Old Testament (1 Cor 10:4) but also ontologically: he was equal with God (Ph 2:6); "he was rich but became poor for our sake" (2 Cor 8:9). As Son, Jesus was rich, being equal to the Father, possessing the fullness of the Godhead (Col 2:9).

Christ is the wisdom of God (1 Cor 1:24, 30) because God's salvific counsel is made manifest in him. He is the image of his Father (2 Cor 4:4). In Jesus the likeness of God the Father is fully present (Jn 12:45; Col 1:15). For the biblical writers an image (eikon) is not merely a faithful copy, but a visible reproduction, a radiant impression in which the being of the original is exteriorized. In Paul it is closely linked with the idea of glory and is thus a clear expression of the con-substantiality of Christ with the Father in his divinity. Christ is the perfect copy of his Father's nature (Heb 1:3); he is the replica of the Father's substance, like an exact impression made by a seal on clay or wax (Jn 14:9). There is identity of nature yet distinction of persons. Christ is the image by which and in which all things were created (Col 1:15-17), and have been recreated (Rm 8:29) because into his own person is gathered the fullness of the Godhead and of the universe (Col 2:9); he is the pleroma of all possible categories of beings.

In short, Jesus is one of the divine Persons enumerated in the Trinitarian formulas (2 Cor 13:13). To him, Son of God, be glory forever: Amen (Rm 11:36).

Twenty-five

ADORATION OF CHRIST

The Book of Revelation is the gospel, the proclamation and acclamation of the Risen Christ, a gospel of adoration and worship. The liturgy of the Church naturally centers about that event which made it what it is, the redemptive work of Christ. This appears in hymnic form throughout Revelation: 1:4-7, 4:8, 11, 5:9-14, 7:9-17, 11:15-18, 12:10-12, 15:2-4, 19:1-8. These doxologies celebrating Christ's glory, along with that of the Father, are among the most ancient manifestations of Christian worship and express a constant New Testament theme (Heb 13:21; Rm 9:5; 2 Tm 4:18; 1 P 4:11; 2 P 3:18). They are the New Testament counterpart of the Old Testament hymns of anticipated triumph (e.g., Ps 27, 28, 46, etc.). Nowhere else in the New Testament are the personal activities of Christ present in his Church, the glories of his heavenly life, or the possibilities of his future manifestation so magnificently set forth. Christ shows the prerogatives of God and is glorified as such. Thus with Paul, the author of Revelation has seen "the revelation of the glory of God in the face of Jesus Christ" (2 Cor 4:6), and with John he knows that whoever has seen the Son has seen the Father (Jn 14:9).

A first doxology occurs in the prologue to Revelation (1:4-6). "To him who loves us and has washed away our sins with his blood, who has made us a royal nation of priests in the service of his God and Father, to him be glory and power forever and ever! Amen." This is the kind of language used in worship and like the other doxologies may possibly represent early Christian hymns. Christ loves us; this will not be repeated in such direct terms. Christ's love is perpetual and goes beyond the historical event of the redemption completed once and for all.

In 4:8-11 we have an angelic liturgy in which the four animals representing the created world sing a hymn in honor of God the creator and ruler of the world and human history: "Holy, Holy, Holy is the Lord God, the Almighty; he was, he is, and he is to come." God's holiness is the divine transcendency, God's separation from the profane, his supremacy in all domains and complete separation from all evil. The 24 elders, God's angelic princely guard, join in saying: "You are our Lord and our God, you are worthy of glory and honor and power, because you made all the universe and it was only by your will that everything was made and exists." The living creatures praised the essential nature of God, the elders the glory of God in his works.

In Rv 5:9-10 the creatures and elders sing the praises of the Lamb, Christ's main title throughout the Apocalypse. And all the hosts of heaven take up the chorus: "The Lamb that was sacrificed is worthy to be given power, riches, wisdom, strength, honor, glory, and blessing" (12). This song in celebration of the redemption answers to the song of creation in 4:11. The work of God and his glory have been completed thanks to Christ's sacrifice.

The whole of creation, without any exception, now joins in the great canticle of praise crying: "To the one who is sitting on the throne and to the Lamb, be all praise, honor, glory, and power, forever and ever" (13). All created beings, angels and men, acclaim God and the Lamb together after the separate doxologies. This conjunction of God and the Lamb, which recurs frequently, represents an advanced christology; the same worship is addressed to God and to the Lamb. This conception of the Lamb on the throne of the universe is one of the most sublime in the Bible. It suggests that love is the strongest power in the world.

In 7:9-17 we are given an anticipatory glimpse of the bliss of heaven. The Church is presented as celebrating a perpetual feast of Tabernacles. The martyrs stand for the type-believers, the ideal Christians. "They shouted in a loud voice, Victory to our God who sits on the throne and to the Lamb" (10). Salvation has here the nuance of victory and is the keynote of their worship, paid to the source of their deliverance. God and his Christ are both hailed as Savior, the very title wrongly ascribed to the emperor. This hymn of joy will recur at the fall of the dragon (12:10) and of Babylon (19:1). The whole court of heaven now joins the acclamation of the saints: "Amen. Praise and glory and wisdom and thanksgiving and honor and power and strength to our God forever and ever. Amen" (11-12). Thus placed at the beginning and the end of the doxology, the Amen frames the hymn and expresses full association of all the angels with the praise of the elect. The saved are described as having washed their robes white in the blood of the Lamb (14). Blood is a way of referring to the cross of Christ through which multitudes have had their soiled lives purified and have been assured of God's forgiveness. The Christian cooperates with divine grace by repentance and faith and the use of the sacraments and by vigilance and victory over sin. In the heavenly feast of Tabernacles there is no need to construct booths; God himself will be our tabernacle (15).

The blast of the seventh trumpet (11:15) is followed by a burst of triumph and praise from unspecified voices in heaven and from the twenty-four elders announcing the divine victory. "The kingdom of the world has become the kingdom of our Lord and he will reign forever and ever" (15). The triumph over diabolical powers has removed all obstacles to the effective reign of God over the world. This consummation of salvation history, the essential object of God's promises, is so certain that its realization is expressed in the past tense. The song of the elders describes the final retribution. "We give thanks to you, Almighty Lord God, He-is-and-He-was, for using your great power and beginning your reign. The nations were seething with rage and now the time has come for your own anger and for the dead to be judged and for your servants the prophets, for the saints and all who worship you, small and great, to be rewarded. The time has come to destroy those who are destroying the earth" (17-18).

Rv 12:7-12 describes Michael's victory over the dragon, the primeval serpent known as the devil or Satan who has deceived all the world (9). The devil is a beaten foe; his fury springs from the fact that he knows that his time is short (12). "Then I heard a voice shout from heaven, Victory and power and empire forever have been won by our God and all authority for his Christ, now that the persecutor, who accused our brothers day and night before our God, has been brought down. They have triumphed over him by the blood of the Lamb and by the witness of their martyrdom because even in the face of death they would not cling to life" (10-11). The hymn praises the triumph of God and of his Christ. Michael's victory is simply the heavenly and symbolic counterpart of the earthly reality of the Cross. "Let the heavens rejoice and all who live there; but for you, earth and sea, trouble is coming because the devil has gone down to you in a rage, knowing that his days are numbered" (12). The more fully the Church gains the victory over sin, the more she must expect to be persecuted. It is not worth-while to persecute a dead Church.

The hymn of Moses and of the Lamb (15:1-4) serves as a consoling interlude, interrupting the development of the vision of the seven bowls of plagues which are the definitive manifestation of God's anger. The hymn of Moses (Ex 15) celebrated Israel's triumph over Pharaoh. Here the conquerors of the beast celebrate the justice of God in punishing the wicked persecutors. The two dispensations are thus brought together, the triumph over Pharaoh typifying the Savior's triumph over death and sin. "How great and wonderful are your works, Lord God Almighty; just and true are all your ways, King of nations. Who would not revere and praise your name, O Lord? You alone are holy, and all the pagans will come and adore you for the many acts of justice you have shown" (3-4). The song is a hymn to the omnipotence and justice of the God of salvation history. He is absolute Master; all his interventions are perfect, especially the redemption accomplished by the Lamb and the consummation of history soon to be described in the vision of the seven bowls (ch. 16). The second part of the hymn tells of the repercussions that these *magnalia Dei* will have among the nations which will acknowledge the glory of God (21:24-26, 22:2). The canticle contains no allusion to Moses or to the Lamb. The introductory reference to them (3) is typical and implicit in the context. Unlike the song of Exodus which was one of triumph over enemies, this one is in praise of God. Attention is concentrated entirely on the Lord, the Master of all.

The heavenly, triumphal canticles of joy contained in 19:1-10 were prescribed in 18:20 and are in sharp contrast with the somber earthly tones of the lamentations over the ruins of Babylon contained in chapter 18. The passage consists of two hymns: the first (1-4) is sung by the angels and celebrates God's justice as manifested in the punishment of Babylon considered as already accomplished; the second (5-9), sung by the entire Church, affords us a glimpse of the wedding of the Lamb as a more immediate prospect. This wedding symbolizes the union of the Messiah with the community of the elect.

"After this I seemed to hear the great sound of a huge crowd in heaven singing, Alleluia! Victory and glory and power to our God! He judges fairly, he punishes justly, and he has condemned the famous prostitute who corrupted the earth with her fornication; he has avenged his servants that she killed. They sang again, Alleluia, the smoke of her will go up forever and ever" (1-3). The whole Church now joins its song of praise to that of the angels, elders and the four animals. "Alleluia! the reign of the Lord our God Almighty has begun" (6). The Church's hymn has the same theme as that of the angels, but whereas the angels' song emphasized the negative aspect, the punishment and destruction of Babylon, the present hymn treats of the inauguration of the kingdom of God. "Let us be glad and joyful and give praise to God, because this is the time for the marriage of the Lamb." This motif including the overwhelming joy of the Church is an anticipation of the book's final vision (20:11-22:5). The theme of marriage uniting God with his people was already well established in the Old Testament. In the New Testament, it is used to express the vital union between Christ and his Church. The symbol expresses the intimate and indissoluble union with the community that Christ has won by his blood, the establishment of the heavenly kingdom described in 21:9f.. "His bride is ready, and she has been able to dress herself in dazzling white linen, because her linen is made of the good deeds of the saints" (8). The corporate holiness of the Church, fitting her to be a bride, is attained by the individual acts of her members. The doctrine of the communion of saints is contained in and follows from that of the holy, catholic Church.

Briefly and in summary, the doxologies of the Apocalypse in a special way and in agreement with the rest of the book, show the very special relation of the glorified Christ with God. Christ shows the prerogatives of God. He searches the mind and heart of man (2:23). With the Father he gives grace and peace (1:4) and receives the adoration of creatures (5:13). He occupies one throne with God (22:1, 3) and shares his sovereignty (11:15). Christ receives the titles of God: he is the living one (1:17), holy and true (3:7), the Alpha and Omega (22:13). And several Old Testament passages and ideas relative to God are spontaneously applied to Christ. Thus Christ is assimilated to and identified with God, worthy of the same honor and adoration.

Twenty-six

PRAYER TO JESUS

Christian biblical prayer is usually addressed to God the Father, yet the question arises whether Jesus because of his mediation which takes many forms, and because of his central position in prayer, is not also somehow the direct object of prayer. Briefly, this is the thesis. Direct, exclusive prayer is not to be addressed to Jesus; but that is true also of the Father and of the Holy Spirit. Direct non-exclusive prayer to Christ is rightful, because of the unity of nature and action in the divinity which theologians call the interchange of attributes: Christ is both God and man. It is a fact, however, that biblical prayer is seldom addressed directly to Jesus; this is a problem that demands some investigation in the light of the progressive revelation of Christ's divinity.

During his ministry Jesus manifests the powers of an extra-ordinary wonder-worker. The crowds come to him, beg and implore him, trusting in his help, like the suppliant who has recourse to God in prayer. Actually these appeals are directed essentially to the man who is considered as endowed with a special power to do good by wonderful means (Mt 14:30).

Prostration before a person does not necessarily imply adoration; it is not only a posture for prayer but also an initial salutation expressing respect by falling down before a person and kissing his feet, the hem of his garment, or the ground. Jesus teaches that this attitude, as a mark of adoration, is reserved for God alone (Mt 4:9-10). During his earthly life prostration is the attitude of those who desire something from Jesus (Mt 8:2); it expresses veneration for a holy person, a prophet or wonder-worker (Lk 5:8). There is no adoration either when the disciples or others, prostrate before Jesus, proclaim him the expected Messiah, the Christ, the Son of David, or even the Lord (Mt 2:8, 20-20). On Palm Sunday the crowds shout, "Hosanna to the Son of David" (Mt 21:9). Hosanna originally was a Hebrew invocation addressed to God (Ps 118:25) meaning "O save"; later is was used, as here, as a cry, a shout of joyous acclamation. The same is true when people apply to Jesus the Messianic texts of the Old Testament (Mt 23:29) or even the title Son of God (Mt 14:33) which is used frequently in the Old Testament for adoptive sonship. Nor does the fact that angels minister to Jesus (Mt 4:11) imply adoration. All this is the normal expression of veneration and respect due to a special individual who, in the case of Jesus, is constantly seen in a better light.

The prostrations before Jesus after the Resurrection usually have the same meaning (Mt 28:9, 17) yet one might suspect some incipient notion of worship (Lk 24:52). In fact, in relation to the risen Christ we begin to find terms similar to those used for God and consequently the notion of worship slowly emerges. At the name of Jesus the whole universe bends the knee, as to one whose state is divine (Ph 2:6, 19); the angels worship him as the first-born of the Father (Heb 1:6, cf. Ps 97:7). He is given the title Lord (*Kyrios*) which is the Septuagint translation of the divine name Yahweh in the Old Testament: "Every tongue should acclaim Jesus Christ as Lord" (Ph 2:11).

Paul uses *Kyrios*, of course, for Yahweh of the Old Testament, especially in passages where he quotes Old Testament texts. But the absolute *Kyrios* becomes Paul's title of predilection for Jesus. This absolute use is well attested in the Hellenistic world. *Lord* was a sovereign title for the Roman Emperor. And though it primarily denoted his political and juridical authority, it also carried the nuance of his divinity. Paul's usage of the title for Jesus is not really a borrowing of this current usage but an inheritance from the early Palestinian liturgical tradition.

The first credal formulas (Rm 10:9; 1 Cor 12:3) point in that direction, as also the climax of the hymn to Christ in Ph 2:6-11 where Christ is given the name Lord, the name that is above all names. The proclamation "Jesus is Lord" is the essence of the

Christian creed (2 Cor 4:5, Col 2:6). Once Jesus became the object of worship, given the absolute use of *Kyrios* in the Septuagint for Yahweh and the contemporary application of the title to gods and rulers, *Kyrios* was the ideal title for Paul's missionary efforts among the Gentiles (Ac 11:20).

The use of *Kyrios* for Jesus in the early Church bestowed on him the ineffable name of Yahweh. In effect it suggests that Jesus is on a par with Yahweh himself. This equality is spelled out in detail in the hymn in Ph 2:6-11; the reason why the name given to Jesus is above every name is that it is Yahweh's own name. This is the early Church's way of expressing its faith in the divinity of Christ. The title *Kyrios* ascribes to both Yahweh and Jesus a dominion over creation and a right to the adoration of all creation. In echoing Is 45:23, Ph 2:10 implies this very idea: what Isaiah said of Yahweh is now applied to Christ: "To me every knee shall bow, every tongue shall swear." This usage is a clear indication of the divine character that is meant to be understood by the title Lord.

In Jn 20:28 Thomas says, "My Lord and My God," speaking the language that became the common confession concerning Jesus (Ac 2:36, Ti 2:13). He is Lord because in virtue of his elevation to the Father's right hand, he rules over the kingdom in this fullness of time.

The formula "to invoke the name of Jesus" does not necessarily suppose that a formal prayer is addressed to him. It is to give Jesus the name Lord, to recognize his Lordship. The two expressions "to invoke the name of the Lord" and "to confess that Jesus is Lord" are practically equivalent but they do imply worship and prayer. Christ's name is powerful and it is invoked in all necessity for his intervention. In his name the disciples themselves perform miracles (Ac 3:6). To invoke the name of Jesus is to recognize his intimate union with God, it is to profess belief in his mission, it is to participate in his work of salvation. Christians (Ac 9:14) are "the holy people who call on the name of our Lord Jesus Christ" (Rm 16:16), particularly those who believe in him and have recourse to him.

Jesus is at the center of worship because in him dwells the

fullness of the divinity bodily (Col 2:9). In him glory is given to God and by him God makes himself accessible to all who invoke him (Rm 10:12). The Christian liturgy celebrates in Christ the liberation worked by God through him. Professions of faith, hymns, praise are aimed directly at the historical work realized by Jesus, and consequently either they join him to the Father or they are addressed to him directly (Ep 1:3-13; Col 1:15-20). The expressions of praise, *the doxologies* usually have a liturgical, cultic background and consequently are especially important in the study of the development of the expression of direct prayer or cult to Jesus.

Jewish literature reserved doxologies for God the Father. Paul often betrays his Jewish background by spontaneously uttering a doxology at the climactic mention of God as the Creator, "who is blessed for ever. Amen!" (Rm 1:25). "All that exists comes from him; all is by him and for him. To him be glory for ever. Amen!" (Rm 11:36). These are doxologies to God the Father as the creator, sustainer, and goal of the universe; its source, medium, and end; the efficient, sustaining, and final cause.

The work of our salvation, the new creation, is according to the Father's plan and is realized in time by his Son; praise is then also addressed to Jesus at the same time as the Father in many doxologies, sometimes indirectly with the prepositions through or in, sometimes directly. "Give glory therefore to him through Jesus Christ for ever and ever. Amen" (Rm 16:27). "Glory to him from generation to generation in the Church and in Christ Jesus for ever and ever" (Ep 3:21). In Revelation we find, "To the one who is sitting on the throne and to the Lamb, be all praise, honor, glory, and power for ever and ever" (5:13). "Victory to our God who sits on the throne and to the Lamb" (7:10). These doxologies celebrating Christ's glory along with that of the Father are among the most ancient manifestations of Christian worship and are part of a constant New Testament theme.

Paul rarely gives Jesus the title God (Rm 9:5, Ti 2:13) but the same is true of the rest of the New Testament, although we do find clear instances in the later writings (Jn 1:1, 20:28; Heb 1:8-9; P 1:1). Consequently Paul rarely addresses a doxology to Christ alone but there are some: "Christ who is above all, God for ever blessed. Amen!" (Rm 9:5). "To him be glory for ever and ever. Amen!" (2 Tm 4:18). "Through Christ to whom be glory for ever and ever. Amen!" (Heb 13:21). And such doxologies are not found only in the Pauline writings. "To him be glory in time and in eternity. Amen!" (2 P 3:18). "To him be glory and power for ever and ever. Amen!" (Rv 1:6).

The Trinitarian doxology, as we know it, is the perfect expression of worship, the three divine persons being treated on a basis of equality as is stressed in the Athanasian Creed: "Glory to the Father, and to the Son, and to the Holy Spirit." 2 Cor 13:13 is just about the only one found in the Scriptures: "The grace of the Lord Jesus Christ, the love of God and the fellowship of the Holy Spirit be with you all." This formula, probably derived from liturgical usage, is the richest and most instructive of Paul's benedictions at the end of his letters. The second person assumed our human nature and by his death and resurrection is the author of all grace by which we are justified and sanctified. The love of the Father is the ultimate source of this grace for "the Father so loved the world that he sent his only Son" (Jn 3:16). And all graces are communicated to us by the Holy Spirit who is the distributor of all sanctifying graces (Gal 5:22) and of all special charisma (1 Cor 12:4). The order is significant: the grace of Christ leads one toward the love of God and the love of God when actualized through the Spirit produces fellowship with God and man.

The basic reason for Paul's rare use of the term God for Jesus, as also for the few references to his divinity, is that for Paul God (*O theos*) is referred to the Father. "For us there is one God, the Father, from whom all things come and from whom we exist" (1 Cor 8:6). But he immediately adds: "And there is one Lord, Jesus Christ, through whom all things come and through whom we exist." In Second Corinthians (13:13) Scripture comes quite close to our official liturgical doxology: "Glory to the Father, and to the Son, and to the Holy Spirit," which gives recognition to each divine person.

There are interesting instances where direct prayer and worship of Christ surface in the course of this liturgical evolution.

Ep 5:19, "singing and chanting to the Lord in your hearts," is one of the rare texts in which there is mention of prayer addressed to Christ, the Lord. The phrase is all the more noteworthy when one sees that in the parallel Col 3:16 it is God who is the object of the congregation's praise. One also can hardly fail to remember how Pliny the Younger, in his description of the first Christians, speaks of "a hymn sung to Christ as to God," referring evidently to the primitive liturgy.

Stephen's prayer at the moment of his death is addressed to Jesus: "As they were stoning Stephen, he prayed, 'Lord Jesus, receive my spirit' " (Ac 7:59). The prayer of Jesus at his death (Lk 23:46) is repeated by the martyr and it is now addressed to Jesus as Lord. As in Christ's case, prayer and action are joined by Stephen in the same sacrifice. Stephen's prayer prolongs his liturgical confession of faith and expresses the meaning of his martyrdom.

Finally, the liturgical Aramaic acclamation maranatha occurs under two complementary forms. In 1 Cor 16:22, "The Lord is coming" (*maran atha*) is a profession of faith and expresses the hope that the Parousia will not be long delayed. In Rv 22:20, "Amen, come Lord" (*marana tha*) is a prayer expressive of the Christian's longing for the Parousia. It implies that God's kingdom has definitely come on earth, that all God's promises have been kept, and looks forward to the final paradisiac period. This prayer for the total realization of God's salvific plan is well addressed to Jesus whose final coming will be its main feature.

Twenty-seven

IN CHRIST JESUS

John but especially Paul suggest the different facets of Christ's influence on the life of Christian believers by using pregnant prepositional phrases to express the intimate union between Christ and the Christian. Four of these phrases deserve special attention: through Christ, into Christ, with Christ and in Christ.

The preposition *through* denotes the mediation of Christ in his earthly ministry (1 Th 5:9), in his present state as the risen, exalted Lord (Rm 1:5) or at the Parousia, when God who raised Jesus and made him Lord will through Jesus raise us up also with him (1 Th 4:14; 1 Cor 6:14). Thus is opened the path that leads to the Christian experience of union in Christ and eventually of eternal salvation with Christ.

The preposition *into* expresses the movement towards Christ implied in the initial Christian experiences of belief or baptism. The biblical phrase for belief is literally *on* God or Christ suggesting not only the object of belief but also its surety and foundation. Abandoning his original condition in Adam (1 Cor 15:22) and his natural inclination in the flesh (Rm 7:5), the Christian is incorporated into Christ by faith and baptism (Rm 6:3; Gal 3:27).

The preposition *with* in St. Paul expresses a double relationship of the Christian to Christ: either the identification of the Christian with the redemptive acts of Christ's historical risen life (the Christian suffers with Christ, dies with him, is buried, raised and glorified with him) or the Christian's association with Christ in eschatological glory. Paul has coined over thirty compound words, using the preposition *with*, to describe the different phases or aspects of our union with Christ. They constitute barbarisms and it is impossible to translate them into the vernacular except by circumlocution yet they express perfectly the new reality which Paul wanted to describe. Notice that the Christian is never said to be born with Christ, to be baptized with Christ or tempted with Christ. These events of the life of Christ are not considered significant in Pauline soteriology, even if it is Christ's life as a whole which is redemptive. In St. Paul our mystical union with Christ originates at the high moment of redemption, the time of the Passion, and from that moment on it is continuous and the *communicatio idiomatum* between Christians and Christ is henceforth complete. All that Christ did, he did by right and potentially with us who are his members. This juridical identification considered in God (*ordo intentionis*) is called predestination; in *Christ* (*ordo executionis, de jure, in causa meritoria*) it is merit and redemption; identification becomes an actual fact, a reality in us (*ordo executionis, in recipiente de facto*) by baptism and the Eucharist which incorporate us in Christ. This incorporation thrives on faithful correspondence to grace and is consummated in the glory of heaven.

The phrase *with Christ* refers to the two poles of the Christian experience, as Paul puts it in Rm 6:8: "We believe that having died with Christ, we shall return to life with him." Identified with Christ in the work of redemption, the Christian hopes to be associated with Christ in eschatological glory. It is his destiny to be with Christ (1 Th 4:14). In the meanwhile he lives in Christ: "I live now not with my own life but with the life of Christ who lives in me" (Gal 2:20).

The expression *in Christ* or its equivalents recur constantly as a favorite theme in St. Paul's writings. The preposition *in* indicates a very close connection and according to the matter treated can indicate unions of a totally different character, from the union that exists between an action and its velocity, to the union between Christ and those who are his. Especially in Paul or John it designates the close personal relation of Christ who is in the Father (Jn 14:10) and of Christians who are or abide in Christ (Jn 14:20).

Paul has the most varied expressions for this new life principle, union with Christ. It is life in Christ: the Christian must consider himself dead to sin but alive for God in Christ (Rm 6:11). It is love in Christ: no created thing can ever come between the Christian and the love of God made visible in Christ Jesus, our Lord (Rm 8:39). It is the grace which is given in Christ (1 Cor 1:4), freedom in Christ (Gal 2:4), blessing in Christ (Gal 3:14), unity in Christ (Gal 3:28), incorporation into Christ's body through the one Spirit (1 Cor 12:13).

The formula *in Christ* is especially common with verbs that denote a conviction, hope, or strong Christian sentiment (e.g., Ph 4:2). This is the strong sense of deep Christian living. But also apart from such verbs, it occurs in many passages with verbs and nouns of the most varied sort, often without special emphasis, to indicate the scope within which something takes place, or simply to designate something as Christian, something done in a Christian manner, e.g., to marry in the Lord is to marry a Christian (1 Cor 7:39).

The phrase *in Christ* must not be understood in some vague, spatial, mystical sense of the glorified Christ somehow identified with the Spirit, as some atmosphere in which Christians are bathed. The Christian is not in Christ as a bird in the air or a fish in the sea; rather he is in Christ as borne along in a stream of vital influence to which, more or less fully, he yields himself and through which the Lord is making all that he is himself willing to become.

The phrase in Christ and its equivalents have a great variety of connotations. Thus the phrase *in the Lord* implies Christ's present, sovereign intervention and dominion in the life of the Christian. The title Lord denotes the influence of the risen Lord in practical and ethical areas of Christian conduct. Thus Paul tells the Christian to be in the Lord, that is, publicly and practically, what he really is in Christ, that is, privately and personally, thus stressing the much neglected interior and personal aspect of Christian living.

The phrase in Christ is frequently used in an instrumental sense when it applies to the historical, earthly activity of Christ. Thus we are justified "through the free gift of his grace by being redeemed in Christ Jesus" (Rm 3:24). Usually, however, the phrase in Christ expresses the close union of Christ and the Christian, a living together in intimate association and union. If any man is in Christ he is a new creature (2 Cor 5:17), a new man created in Christ (Ep 2:15). The living acts of the Christians somehow become the acts of Christ and so the vital union can also be expressed as "Christ in me" (Gal 2:20) or as Christ living in our hearts through faith (Ep 3:17). It follows that one belongs to Christ (2 Cor 10:7) or is of Christ (Phm 1:1; Ep 4:1).

The phrase in Christ is thus especially dynamic in meaning, expressing the influence of Christ on the Christian who is incorporated into him. The phrase has then also ecclesial (Ep 1:10) and even eschatological dimensions. God raised us up and already gave us a place in heaven, in Christ Jesus (Ep 2:6). The resurrection and triumph of Christians in heaven is considered as actually existing, so sure is the certitude of our hope.

Briefly, the phrase in Christ points to Christ as the reason for our election, the final causality. Christ is the center of unity and harmony, in him were created all things in heaven and on earth (Col 1:16) and in him all things are brought together under one head (Ep 1:10). In Christ is the keynote of the epistle to the Ephesians. The whole letter shows Christ regenerating and regrouping under his authority, and bringing back to God, the whole world corrupted and broken up by sin, the world of men and even the angelic world.

Some exemplary causality is also included since it is to resemble Jesus that we are elected. We were predestined to become true images of God's Son, so that his Son might be the eldest of many brothers (Ep 8:29). The glory which Christ as the image of God possesses by right (2 Cor 4:4) is progressively communicated to the Christian (2 Cor 3:18) until his body is itself clothed in the image of the heavenly man (1 Cor 15:49).

Efficient causality is also expressed since Jesus is the means of our sanctification. In him we have redemption, through his blood we gain our freedom, the forgiveness of our sins (Ep 1:7). And finally and especially quasi-formal causality. It is union with Jesus through charity which makes us holy and acceptable to God (Ep 1:3-4).

The phrase in Christ involves the unity of Christ with his Father, of Christ and Christians, and of Christians among themselves.

Jesus claimed, "The Father and I are one" (Jn 10:30). In the context the primary meaning is that the Son's power is not other than the Father's. Father and Son are one in mind, will, and action. This unity presupposes the even more essential one of which John (1:1) speaks: "The Word was God." The unity of the Godhead is indicated by "one"; Jesus does not say that he and the Father are "at one" but are one thing. The distinction of persons is clear from "are." As St. John Chrysostom puts it, "If the power is the same so is the being."

Say Jesus and you have to say God. This unity between the Father and the Son is not, however, merely cosmological or metaphysical; the moral relationships of love and obedience are primary (Jn 10:17). But essential relationship (1:1) is also implied and is what enrages the Jews (10:33). Unclouded openness of the mind of the Son to the mind of the Father was the essence of his being; a profound inner sense of harmony and indeed unity of will.

The unity of Christ and Christians is the essential meaning of the phrase "in Christ" as was sufficiently shown above. By baptism and the Eucharist the Christian is so closely united to Christ that his life, sufferings, and death can be attributed to Christ living in him and being glorified in him (Ph 1:20).

The unity of the Christian community is based on the union of each believer with God in Christ. "What we have seen and heard we are telling you so that you too may be in union with us, as we are in union with the Father and his Son, Jesus Christ" (1 Jn 1:3). This union is the idea most central to John's mysticism (Jn 15:1-6). It is expressed in different ways. A Christian lives in God and God lives in him (1 Jn 2:5, 6); a Christian is begotten by God, has new life from him (2:29); a Christian is from God, is his child (2:16); the Christian knows God (2:3). This union with God shows itself in a person's faith and in his love for the brothers (1:7).

God is in Christians as the principle of their new life. And since God is light (1:5), righteousness (2:29), and love (4:8, 16) whoever lives in union with God must live a life of light, virtue, and love, and keep God's commandments, especially the commandment of loving all human beings (2:10-11). Faith and love are thus the visible evidence of true union with God (1:6-7).

Finally, in many instances the phrases "in Christ" and "in the Spirit" are interchangeable. They are applied to faith, love and peace. To be in the Spirit is to be in Christ for the corporate Christ is the Spirit's realm or sphere of operation (Rm 8:9). Hence we are sealed in Christ or in the Spirit (Ep 4:30) and sanctified in either (Rm 15:16; 1 Cor 1:2). Yet like all synonyms the two expressions have a nuance of meaning. The interchange becomes impossible when in Christ refers to our election by God (Rm 8:39) or to Christ as the second Adam (Rm 3:24), that is, when Christ is represented as Messiah and as Mediator between God and man.

Notice also that the same force is possessed by the expression *Christ in us*. Christ inhabits our bodies through his Holy Spirit as the parallelism of "Christ in you" and "the Spirit of Christ in you" proves. Christ lives in the community as well as in the individual; he grows in stature in the same measure as the believer grows in faith (Gal 4:19). He even comes to replace our earthly nature, the old man in us, with a new personality (Gal 2:19-20).

To be complete a word must be said about the Pauline idea of *pleroma*. In Christ is the fullness of being, that is, the fullness both of God (Col 2:9) and of all that exists through God's creative power (Col 1:13-20). The Church is the fullness of Christ (Ep 1:23). It continues, expresses Christ; it develops all the possibilities of sanctification he possesses. Without her the mystical Christ would be incomplete as a head without a body. The Church is the fulfillment or ideal of divine graces, the fulfillment in which is realized the grace of the head. Finally, Christ who is filled with the divine life fills Christians with it (Ep 3:14-23), enters the fullness of the total Christ and even helps to build it up (Col 1:24). Briefly, Christ is the sacrament of God, the Church the sacrament of Christ, and the Christian the sacrament both of the Church and of Christ.

Twenty-eight

COMMUNITY PRAYER

The New Testament is especially rich in references to community prayer. The Christian is not alone, he does not live in isolation; he is a member of a community, of a body whose head is Jesus Christ. In the primitive Christian community goods and needs, apostolic duties and final destiny, practically everything was considered from the viewpoint of the community. That is why Christian prayer, even when it is personal, always transcends the private domain. The formula taught us by Jesus (Mt 6:9-13) is a communitarian prayer with *us* as the agents. The collective character of the Lord's prayer is noteworthy. Even in private prayer we cannot forget our brethren or isolate ourselves. We must rather like to feel united one to another, as disciples of the same Master, sons of the same Father.

Moreover, private prayer which is presented as an acclamation (Mt 11:25; Lk 1:46) has by the very fact a collective bearing. By their very nature praise, and even more intercession, go beyond the level of the individual.

The first Christians lived in common and prayed in common (1 Cor 14:13). The book of Acts presents not so much praying individuals as praying communities, inspired by the prayer in common in the Temple (Ac 3:1). In Acts 13:2 the term used for Christian prayer (offering worship to the Lord) puts Christian prayer on a level with the sacrificial worship of the old law.

The Acts (6:4) show how the Apostles handed over to deacons the daily distribution of food so that they themselves could continue to specialize in prayer and the service of the word. When the community met for public worship, the Apostles had two functions: they recited the prayers and were responsible for the catechesis of the people, the doctrinal elaboration of the good news.

The early Christian community, including Mary the mother of Jesus, is presented as joining in continuous prayer (Ac 1:14). Prayer is part of the description of the life of the first Christian community: "These remained faithful to the teaching of the Apostles, to the brotherhood and to the prayers" (Ac 2:42).

There are many examples in the Acts of the constant prayer Jesus recommended (Mt 6:5) and practised (Mt 14:23). There is the prayer in common presided over by the Apostles (Ac 1:14, 4:24-30, 6:4) with the breaking of the bread as the central ceremony (2:42, 46, 20:7, 11).

There is also the prayer for special occasions like the election and ordination to office in the Church: for Matthias (1:24) and for the deacons. These were presented to the Apostles "who prayed and laid their hands on them" (6:6). The laying of the hands is a prayerful gesture expressing the donation and reception of a gift; Jesus blessed the children (Mk 10:16), healed with a touch (Mk 6:5); the Spirit is given to the baptized by the laying of the hands (Ac 8:17, 19:6) and by this gesture men are set aside for special tasks in the Church (6:6) by those in authority. After fasting and prayer (Ac 13:3) the community commends to God's grace the newly chosen missionaries, Barnabas and Saul, by laying hands on them. The gesture in this case is a prayer asking God's help for the new work of evangelization. The Apostles' prayer in time of persecution is also noteworthy (Ac 4:24-30).

Paul asks his communities to pray for one another and for the progress of evangelization: "Pray for us especially, asking God to show us opportunities for announcing the message and proclaiming the mystery of Christ. . . Pray that I may proclaim it as clearly as I ought" (Col 4:3).The members of the communities join forces by prayer in the struggle they sustain: "I beg you, brothers, by our Lord Jesus Christ and the love of the Spirit, to help me through my dangers by prayer for me" (Rm 15:30). "You must all join in the prayers for us: the more people there are asking for help for us, the more will be giving thanks when it is granted to us" (2 Cor 1:11), "the more thanksgiving there will be, to the glory of God" (2 Cor 4:15).

There is special efficacy for prayer in common: "I tell you solemnly once again, if two of you on earth agree to ask anything at all, it will be granted to you by my Father in heaven. For where two or three meet in my name, I shall be there with them" (Mt 18:19-20). The reason for the efficacy of the prayer of the community is the presence of Jesus whose prayer the Father always hears (Jn 11:42). In Judaism the Rabbis taught that God is present in power wherever a group of believers is gathered for the sake of the law. In the new dispensation Christ takes the place of the law; wherever a group is gathered for his sake, in his name, he himself, the presence of God among us, the Emmanuel (Mt 1:23), is there. The abiding presence of Christ is a reality which forms the basis of Matthew's ecclesiology (Mt 28:20). In fact, his gospel closes with a return to the prophecy of Emmanuel. The phrase promises God's powerfully active assistance; no mere static presence, but a dynamic force for the accomplishment of a mission (Ex 3:12; Jos 1:5).

Christian community prayer was at first expressed in the Temple, in the official framework of the Jewish religion, on feast days, and each day at the specified times. Jesus and his disciples took part in it (Jn 5:1; Ac 2:46). Soon the first day of the Jewish week, the Lord's day (Rv 1:10), so called in memory of the Resurrection, became the day of the Christian community's liturgical reunion for the Eucharist, the breaking of the bread (Ac 20:7).

Everyone shares in the liturgical community prayer from time immemorial by answering Amen. The word occurs first of all in the Old Testament to indicate the participation, the assent of the individual, who thus makes his own the prayer of the community. "Blessed be Yahweh, the God of Israel from all eternity and forever. And let all the people say, Amen" (1 Ch 16:36). Amen is a one word kerygmatic summary of faith and prayer. It is a Hebrew verbal adjective and means first of all, sure, faithful. In a derived adverbial sense it means surely, certainly, no doubt. It is used to confirm the validity of an agreement, a covenant or saying, and declares readiness to bear its consequences. A solemn agreement will often be underlined by repetition at the end. "Then Ezra blessed Yahweh, the great God, and all the people raised their hand and answered, Amen, Amen" (Ne 8:6), in assent to the renewal of the Covenant. Amen is often used at the conclusion of a doxology or prayer. Thus we find it as the conclusion of the first four books of Psalms: "Blessed be Yahweh, the God of Israel, from all eternity and forever! Amen, Amen!" (Ps 41:43, 72:19, 89:51, 106:48).

Our Lord's use of amen, amen, as a preface to a statement (Jn 1:51) is peculiar to him and gives special emphasis to what he is asserting. He has heard from the Father all that he says (Jn 8:26, 28), and the amen with which he introduces what he says assures us that God guarantees the truth of his statements. He is the Word of God. "It is through him that we answer amen to the praise of God" (2 Cor 1:20); he is the amen of our faith (Rv 3:14), its guarantee. In him the divine promises have found their fulfillment. Hence the conclusion of the Eucharistic prayer, the Church's great community prayer: "through him, with him, and in him, all glory and honor is yours, almighty Father, for ever and ever. Amen!"

Twenty-nine

PRAYER IN THE GARDEN

"I can pray to God anywhere. In fact, I often feel closer to God in a garden than in the cold, dark halls of a great, empty cathedral, or even than in the misty, incense filled Church, jammed with the Sunday crowd of worshippers." Such sentiments are often voiced today by people who shy away from form and structure, in favor of what they like to qualify as the freedom of the children of God. I suppose that on a wintry night they are thinking nostalgically of the long, warm, lazy, green days of summer; of white thatched cottages where roses ramble and honeysuckle climb; of sheltered gardens with columbine, cyclamen, and dogwood blossoms, where humming bees work among lovely blooms and the air is heavy with the scent of many flowers. I doubt that the thought includes gardens wet and muddy, cold and dismal, stripped, windswept, and water-logged. I submit that their reaction is simply romantic and unrealistic; that it shies away from taking in the whole picture of life; that it is a long way from the heart of the gospel.

To the one who would say "I can worship God in the garden, I pray better in the solitude and silence of my privacy" (Mt 6:5-6), I should like to answer first that what Scripture deprecates in that Matthean passage is ostentatious prayer. And then I should like to ask, "But do you pray to God in those conditions? And if you do, is he the God and Father of our Lord, Jesus Christ (2 Cor 1:3)?

The god of the garden (or of the study) is usually a vague, nature-God, who keeps his distance and never troubles you; a nebulous being, a kind of insubstantial merger of color and perfume, warm sunshine, and droning bees, (of cigar smoke and background music). A man leans on the grass in his garden, or on his spade some Sunday evening in summertime (or puffs on his pipe on a cold winter night). He gazes at a splendor of foliage, a symphony of beautiful color and murmurs rhetorically, "Only God can make a tree" and jollies himself that he has worshipped sufficiently. His reflection surely contains some of the admiration which is part of worship, but what a long way still has to be travelled to reach the mountain of God. Should one be satisfied not to progress beyond his mumbling as a child? Paul says, "When I was a child I used to think like a child, and argue like a child; but now I am a man, all childish ways are put behind me" (1 Cor 13:11).

Really, no one can apprehend the essential message of all the trees, until he has come to the place "somewhat ascending" where there stands one tree, bare and leafless, stark and red, outside the city wall; a tree which is for the healing of the nations. Or to the garden of the Resurrection; but even there the essential message will be "He is not here" (Mk 16:6).

Some pleas for a more meaningful worship sound suspiciously like requests that all sense of mystery be destroyed. It is perfectly legitimate to ask that the words make sense, that gestures and postures be capable of reasonable explanation. At the same time care must be taken not to turn the whole exercise into a farce. Some of the results of recent liturgical experimentation are theologically frightening. Christ is more than the need in the man next to me; my interests must go beyond the needs of the poor and under-privileged; my goal cannot be merely the thankful smile of the poor; the human and secular must be coordinated with the sacral and transcendental; my kindly deed cannot be my only prayer.

The table we spread for the poor in our midst will go stale unless we see it organically one with the Messianic banquet of Eucharistic celebration, preparing the unending feast of heaven. It is fashionable to criticize the established Church for its supposed arrogance, selfishness, and lack of concern for the poor. Christ, we are told, died on the cross between two thieves, not on a high altar between two candles. The Church like Christ should be God's suffering servant, working in society like the silent leaven and growing among men as the seed sown in silence. Actually we do not have to choose between Christ on the throne and Christ washing the feet of his disciples. They are both one and the same person, and Christ's mission is falsified if either his human nature or his divine nature are glossed over or minimized. The gospels are a perfect demonstration of this unity in Christ; Mark stresses the humanity of the Son of God, while John emphasizes the divinity of the Son of Man. The point of Christ's deepest humiliation was the revelation of his greatest victory. He reigned and triumphed from the cross.

If at the Eucharistic celebration I have truly met my king and my God, then in the streets of the secular city I shall be able to start spreading the glory of the coming of the Lord. The invitation to come and worship has its counterpart in the commission to go and serve. The love of God finds expression in the love of our neighbor, the one near us who needs our help. Our prayer, like Christ's, should be a transfiguration, a momentary exhilaration preparing us for the Christian mission. While the glory of the Lord still shines around us in prayer, there sounds in our ears the boom of *therefore* and all the obligations that are before us. We cannot face them except by the grace of him who is the source, guide, and goal of all that is. How could we sustain them and not grow weary in well doing, unless we maintain the spiritual glow? Surely, we cannot meet the demands of the hour and recognize the signs of our times without the resources of eternity.

It is often stated that action is prayer, that one finds God in the service of people. This is deceptive over-simplification. There is first a presupposition of service which may be perfectly valid but which bears some examination. How much real service is there in our daily activities? How much self-service, how much triviality which is of no value to anyone? And granting real service of one's neighbor we should realize that the motivation and energy necessary for loving service cannot be maintained without prayer. It is presumptuous to believe that we can sustain true Christian service without the kind of supporting prayer life that Christ himself exemplified and taught.

Prayer is not an alternate to action; it is the inspiration and support for action. Prayer must reach both God and man with love and service. Prayer without action is not enough, and action without prayer will soon wither and die. Action that is prayer results only from prayer. It is true that the one who works prays, provided we pray by and with our work, and always ground our work in the work of prayer. Vatican II puts it this way: "It is of the essence of the Church that she be both human and divine, visible and yet invisibly endowed, eager to act and yet devoted to contemplation, present in this world and yet not at home in it" (SC, no. 2).

The question is being asked today: "Can I be a good Christian (or religious) without making prayer an essential part of my life?" The right answer to this question would be the wrong one. The right answer is, "Of course you cannot," but both question and answer suggest that the Christian life, the priestly life, is an enormous chore, a heap of distasteful obligations to be plowed through and that prayer is one of these burdensome duties. Actually, Christ's yoke is easy and his burden light (Mt 11:30), because his service is perfect freedom (Rm 8:21).

Does a Christian need prayer? What are we saying? Does a young man desperately in love have to meet his girl friend? Does someone who likes sports have to watch the athletes play? Does a music lover have to go to the concert? The real question should be: how can I possibly hold back when the game is on, when the symphony is playing, when the Lord is calling (Rv 3:20)?

It is true that prayer is not always an occasion of unparalleled inspiration and power. There are times when our approach to God in prayer seems more a duty than a delight. I often come to the altar with weary and slow, dragging feet. Yet how thankful we should be for this discipline, so that whatever we may feel, we will be able to say: "I have eaten my bread and Christ dwells in me to nourish, and guide me, and enable me to teach people and bring them the light of the gospel." "I have prayed for you, Simon, that your faith may not fail, and once you have recovered, you in your turn must strengthen your brothers" (Lk 22:32).

Thirty

ST. PETER JULIAN EYMARD AND EUCHARISTIC PIETY

It would clearly be anachronistic to try to read post-conciliar Vatican II meanings in the pious approach that characterized St. Peter Julian Eymard's Eucharistic devotion. Yet one cannot but be impressed by the Saint's deep insights into the Eucharistic mystery even if his favorite watchword, "Jesus is there, then all to him," does appear myopic in view of today's holistic Eucharistic theology.

It must be said, however, that devotion to the Eucharistic presence, as advocated by St. Eymard, represents a real, pemanent value in the Church. Private prayer and meditation before the Blessed Sacrament exposed, Eucharistic apostolate, have objective, lasting worth that will only be strengthened by being rooted into the essential Eucharistic worship of the Church's Mass liturgy.

The Eucharistic charism characteristic of St. Peter Julian Eymard's spirituality may be summed up in his own words describing a special grace he received at Fourviere, France, in 1851. "Our Lord in the Eucharist does not have to glorify his sacrament of love, a religious body who would make this service their end and consecrate to it all their energies. One must be established."

The official realization of this inspiration is to be found in the two Congregations the saint founded. The Constitutions he wrote for his religious offer the clearest concept of his basic spirituality.

"Let all our religious fully understand that they have been chosen and have made profession to serve the divine person of Jesus Christ, our God and King, truly, really and substantially present in the sacrament of his love. They should, therefore, as good and faithful servants of so great a king, make it a point to consecrate unreservedly all their talents and virtues, studies and labors to his greater glory in perfect abnegation of self, fulfilling the words of the Apostle, 'It is no longer I that live, but Christ lives in me'."

"He who has given himself wholly and forever to Jesus Christ for his love and glory ought to live by him. Our religious, therefore, should strive to live in such a way as to be able to receive Holy Communion frequently, and even daily, with real profit."

These fundamental numbers of the Constitutions are of primordial importance, especially the last quoted, as pointing the way for deep integration into post-Vatican II spirituality.

The Saint insists that "the novices learn first of all to live the interior life and to progress therein, for without it they shall labor in vain and fall by the wayside." Their interior life is thus oriented toward its essential source of nourishment, Holy Communion.

Moreover, for St. Peter Julian the private Eucharistic devotion he advocates is closely related to the essential ecclesial Eucharistic worship in several other ways. In particular because of the exercise of the four ends of sacrifice (adoration, thanksgiving, reparation, and petition) which he recommends as a method of prayer and the spirit of the interior life. For him, also, Eucharistic prayer and meditation should be "based on Holy Communion," should "proceed from the grace of Communion." Prayer should be a spiritual communion, an act of union with our Lord. The whole spiritual life may be reduced to these two elements: "sacramental communion and a life of recollection, of union with our Lord."

Holy Communion was St. Eymard's favorite topic, which he treated from practically every viewpoint. In particular, by advocating frequent, even daily Communion, he anticipated later Pontifical directives.

He insisted on the vital intimacy, the very *real union* that sacramental Communion establishes between the faithful soul and Jesus Christ. "Love wants more than common use of goods and life in common; it desires union, personal and vital union. The love of Jesus has created this union of love, which finds its perfection in the union between him and the disciple in sacramental love. Man can love other men by sharing his possessions, by living the same life in common, by corporal or moral union, but never by vital, spiritual union. That is the extent, the power of Jesus' love for man: 'He who eats my flesh and drinks my blood lives in me and I live in him' " (Jn 6:56).

"Holy Communion is the best grace of love and its perfection. ... The union of Jesus Christ with the faithful soul produces a life of virtue and sanctity." "Communion is the religion of love, the very life of love."

Communion is also the principal *means* of Christian sanctity, the nourishment of the life of grace. "It is by the Eucharist that Jesus sanctifies souls, communicates the precious graces of his Passion."

"All education to be complete must come from our Divine Master. Communion teaches truth by truth itself. The Eucharist is the education of Jesus Christ by Jesus Christ."

"Holy Communion is the grace, the model, and the exercise of all the virtues. By it Jesus forms himself in us, his spirit, his virtues. He unites himself to us to communicate his wisdom, his prudence, his divine power."

"The Christian's formation is more rapid at the Cenacle since in the Eucharist all the graces are put to work. Communion is a vital union, a sacramental union of love, the same life in two persons."

"Holy Communion is the fire consuming in a moment the straw of our spiritual infirmities. It is God's fight in us against our concupiscence, against the devil."

St. Eymard considered the Eucharistic sacramental union as the *end and purpose* of all our Lord's mysteries, the end also of the Christian life and virtues. "Holy Communion is the end, the extension of the Incarnation; by it Christ unites himself to each communicant, establishing a community of life. It is also the end of the Redemption since we must eat the divine victim to participate in his sacrifice. The purpose of the Eucharist is transforming union. The communicant becomes a living temple."

"All the graces of faith, all the sacraments lead up to Holy Communion." "Holy Communion must be the goal of piety. It is the supreme act of the love of Jesus Christ for man, the greatest grace he offers. Christian devotion should then be a preparation for Holy Communion or thanksgiving for its reception."

"Holy Communion being the life and reign of our Lord in us, all our virtues and all our works should converge toward this sacrament of love as to its principle and its end." "Communion should become the dominant thought of our mind and of our heart, the end of all study, piety, and virtue." "Live to receive Holy Communion, and receive it to live a holy life."

"*Love of neighbor,* in particular, stands to profit by the grace of Holy Communion. What we must honor in our brother is Jesus Christ himself who dwells in him and comes to him in Holy Communion." "How beautiful in our sight is our neighbor when we see him seated at the same banquet, fed with the same bread of life, loved so generously by Jesus Christ."

St. Peter Julian often mentions the sacred Liturgy in his writings, but he is usually referring to the Roman rubrics, as opposed to the Gallican customs current at his time. He did, however, have a deep appreciation for the *Holy Sacrifice* of the Mass.

"Holy Mass is an act, the most glorious for God, the most holy and salutary for men." "Holy Mass is the highest act of religion that a Christian can offer to God . . . it has the value of the sacrifice of Calvary." "Mass is the greatest act of religion, the most perfect. It is the favorite devotion of the saints."

"Mass has all the merit of Calvary. It makes all graces available, graces of justification, of sanctification, of preservation. It is the best means of exercising love of neighbor, of making reparation for our sins, of helping the souls in Purgatory, of converting sinners, of glorifying the saints."

"Attend the adorable sacrifice of our altars, as if it were offered for the first time on Calvary. Emulate the sentiments of the Blessed Virgin, St. John, and the holy women who were present at the foot of the Cross."

St. Eymard's special grace as a founder was his *faith in the real presence* of Christ in the Eucharist. "The other sacraments give sanctifying grace; the Eucharist contains the author of grace." "The Eucharist is the personal Emmanuel." "It is the true and

substantial possession of the adorable Person of Jesus Christ."
"Faith, like John the Baptist, shows me Jesus, but Jesus resurrected
and glorified." "The Eucharist is the sacrament of love, par excellence. This is its very name. Love is the cause of its institution,
its perpetuity; it is its end."

The *love of Jesus Christ* in the Eucharist was the very heart of
St. Eymard's interior life, and another favorite theme of his
preaching and of his spiritual direction. "In order that the devout
soul may be strengthened in Christ Jesus and always go forward,
it must be nourished with his divine truth and the love of his
goodness; thus shall it progress wisely from truth to love and
from love to virtue; for the proof of love is in the deed."

"The Eucharist is not only the supreme act of our Lord's love,
it is also the summary of all his acts of love, it is even the end of all
the other mysteries of his life." "Can love go further? No, Jesus
Christ cannot give more than himself." "The Eucharist is among
God's gifts what in nature the sun is to the other heavenly bodies."

"Jesus in the Blessed Sacrament is always the good Master who
alone shows the way to heaven, teaches the truth of God, gives
the life of love." "The Eucharist is Jesus Christ become the memorial, the gift, the sensible proof of his love for man." "In the
Eucharistic Jesus Christ loves you truly, personally, perpetually."
"The Eucharist is an actual love, a present love." "Perfect love
must always be living, and actual; such is our Lord's love in the
Blessed Sacrament."

For St. Eymard, in answer to Christ's Eucharistic love, the
Christian's love becomes a principle of life, thought, and action.
"The disciple of Jesus Christ can reach perfection by two ways.
The first is the law of duty; progress is slow to arrive from vir-
tures to love, which is the bond of perfection. This road is long
and laborious. The second way is shorter and more noble; it is
the road of love, but a love that is total and supreme."

"What was the purpose of Jesus Christ in the institution of
the divine Eucharist? It was to obtain man's supreme love. It was
to be loved by man, possess his heart, become the principle of his
life that our Lord instituted the most blessed Sacrament of the
altar. He says so explicitly: he who eats me shall live by me."

A true spirit of love need not rest in a strictly contemplative life; it normally expresses itself spontaneously in the works of the apostolate. St. Eymard, in the following quote written in 1851, appears as a prophet endowed with a truly pastoral and priestly vision. "I have often reflected on the remedies to this universal indifference which in a frightening way is taking hold of so many Catholics and I find only one, the Eucharist, the love of Jesus Eucharistic. The loss of faith comes first from the loss of love, the glacial cold of death, the absence of fire."

"We must get to work, save souls by the Eucharist, awake the world numbed in the sleep of indifference because it does not know the gift of God, Jesus the Eucharistic Emmanuel. This is the torch of love that must be applied to tepid souls who have not established their center of life in Jesus in the holy tabernacle. Any devotion which does not have a tent on Calvary and one near the tabernacle will not produce a solid piety and will never do anything important."

"Devotion to the blessed Sacrament is necessary to awake the slumbering faith of so many who no longer know Jesus Christ because they have forgotten that he is their neighbor, their friend, their God. It is necessary to save society which is dying because family life has disappeared."

Finally, devotion to the *Priesthood* occupies a privileged place in the spirituality of St. Peter Julian Eymard. "Every Christian should honor Jesus Christ in all the members of his divine priesthood." "The priesthood of Jesus Christ must be honored in a spirit of faith, as another Jesus Christ. Jesus continues by his priests the sanctification of men who should see only him in the priest."

"Happy the priest whose days are full before God, who always acts in God's presence, who fears the Lord and His divine justice, who walks in faith and in union with the saints. Happy is he who greatly desires to save his soul and to love Jesus Christ, for whom Jesus Christ is everything. A thousand times happy and blessed is the priest who chains himself by his thoughts and his heart to the Eucharistic tabernacle, and lives a life of union with Jesus Christ present in the blessed Sacrament."

Pope John XXIII on December 9, 1962, in his homily for the

Mass that followed the canonization of St. Peter Julian Eymard, at the close of the first session of Vatican II, summarized the special charism of the new saint in the following words. "His characteristic not, the guiding idea of all his priestly activity, was the Eucharist: Eucharistic worship and apostolate. . . . After his example place always at the center of your thoughts, affections, and works of zeal this incomparable source of all grace, the *Mysterium Fidei*, the Author of Grace, Jesus, the Word Incarnate."

Thirty-one

LIVING THE TOTAL EUCHARISTIC MYSTERY

To celebrate the total Eucharistic mystery is to attempt to assimilate as much as possible the total mystery of our redemption; to commit oneself completely to the work of Christ; to find in our celebration a source of hope for the liberation of man from all tyranny and slavery; to make the Eucharist meaningful for all men, especially the poor, the sufferer, the hungry, the under-privileged, the sinner, the human mass of forgotten people whose hopeless resignation to their fate is easily changed to blind revolt against unavailing structures. Is not the Eucharist meant for and given to the poor and famished, and "for the forgiveness of sins" (Mt 26:28)? Is it not the ultimate manifestation of our Lord's love (Jn 15:1) for the publicans and sinners, the outcasts whom he came to call to salvation (Mk 2:17)? The Eucharistic celebration presses us (2 Cor 5:14) to walk the path of Christ's redemptive death for us men and for our salvation; to live in the light of Christ's resurrection in joy and hope. To be totally authentic and true it must make us attentive to all man's needs, his sufferings, his revolts, his joys and hopes. Attentive to Christ's coming among us, the Eucharist makes us a pilgrim people with hope in the future in spite of the clouds which crowd the sky of the future, hope at least in the light and expectancy of Christ's final, glorious coming at the time of the Parousia.

Our possession of Christ in the Eucharist cannot be separated from God's revelation of himself in the history of salvation and in the life of men, where we find the face of God in the mystery of the Incarnation of God's Word in our human flesh. To be credible for the man of our time, this adventure of Christ must be relived in our daily life, where human history is made and lived. The Eucharist is the emergence of Christ in our human life. Christ by the Incarnation took on our human condition and by means of his Eucharistic body and blood actualizes the mystery of our redemption, inviting the man of good will to constantly closer union with him but also to greater attention to the needs of his human brothers, divinizing him but also hopefully all creation, so that ultimately in Christ and in full liberty "God may be all in all" (1 Cor 15:28).

Briefly, God reveals himself in salvation history as a Covenant God, as a God who binds himself, gets involved in man's fate, and demands man's co-operation in full liberty, even if it is basically refused by the intervention of sin. The promise of a redeemer and its realization by the Incarnation of Jesus Christ accentuate God's original plan for man's salvation. Christ's Incarnation is redemptive, and God's adventure in human land could hardly be better summarized than by the ancient Christian hymn which has been included in Paul's epistle to the Philippians. "Though he was in the form of God, he did not count equality with God a thing to be grasped, but emptied himself, taking the form of a servant, being born in the likeness of men. And being found in human form he humbled himself and became obedient unto death, even death on a cross. Therefore God has highly exalted him and bestowed on him the name which is above every name, that at the name of Jesus every knee should bow, in heaven and on earth and under the earth, and every tongue confess that Jesus Christ is Lord, to the glory of God the Father" (2:6-11).

Such is the good news of salvation for all of us men, and it is in this background that we must place the Eucharist at the end of our Lord's terrestrial mission as the sacrament of salvation today, the sacrament of Christ reaching all men in our time and all times. The Last Supper cannot be isolated from the rest of our Lord's life and be considered as a mere occasional celebration. It is a meal which here below is never finished. The Eucharist must be seen in the totality of God's saving plan and thus will appear as the prolongation of the Incarnation as a prophetic action of Christ as he is about to give his life "for the life of the world" (Jn 6:51).

Our Eucharistic celebration is the actualization, here and now, of the mystery of our redemption in its totality: from the Incarnation to Pentecost, passing by the inseparable mystery of Christ's death and resurrection as the summit of his salvific action, to Christ's final coming at the end of time. The Eucharist joins time with eternity. It actualizes, makes available the past death and resurrection of our Lord; it anticipates the future reality of the final and full glory of Christ's Parousia; it thus finds its novelty, its actuality by joining the past and the future in the present, our own human time, by means of the transformation of bread and wine into the body and blood of Christ, in the liturgical celebration, under the action of God's word and the direction of the Holy Spirit. This emergence of Christ in our human existence is an effective sign of God's gift of salvation which penetrates our human condition and under the action of his Spirit gives us the possibility of renewing all things. The action of Christ in the Eucharist must be understood as a constantly more encompassing hold on all creatures as they are drawn to their ultimate end. This will be achieved with the co-operation of man who is responsible before God for creation's march towards its maker.

The Eucharist, by giving us an actual share in the redemptive Incarnation, as well as in the final coming of our Lord, is essentially prophetic, preparing and shaping the future, while being a presence. It tells us about both the fidelity of Christ in the gift which he makes of himself to his Church, and also his Lordship which demands to be extended to the whole world.

As for the Jews of the time of Jesus, the recall, the memory of an event, did not mean simply to retell history but to live it, or more exactly to relive it; so also for us to celebrate the Eucharist means to live the redemptive mystery in its totality and plenitude, to resurrect it somehow by rendering actual for us all of its effects. It means to recall creation by enjoying all the wonderful works of God; to live the Exodus in the experience of our human freedom. It means to live Christ's commitment to our human condition by his Incarnation and with him to walk the path of love, freely to the end, even death. It is also to share Christ's resurrection and learn how to live as resurrected people; it is to live in expectation of the glorious return of our Lord; it is to learn sharing, joy, and thanksgiving, to be a man of communion; in short, it is to dare for Christ's sake to commit ourselves to the service of mankind and proclaim the hope which our Lord by his Spirit has planted and fosters in our hearts.

Because the Eucharist is the actualization of the mystery of our redemption, it commits us to share in Christ's saving gesture in order that his life may prevail over all the forces of alienation and of death. Our Eucharistic celebration will not ring out completely true if we do not share Christ's conviction that there is no greater love than that a man lay down his life for his friends (Jn 15:13). The Eucharist is the sacrament of redemption and liberation. The Eucharistic bread and wine, fruits of the earth and work of human hands, signify life, joy, liberty. The meal aspect of the sacrament suggests sharing and fraternity. Thus is manifested the total meaning of the Eucharist in a world hungering and thirsting for justice and liberation. By his sacrifice Jesus teaches us love for every man, the value of all men, of every human endeavor, and of every man who has been redeemed by Christ's blood. The Eucharist must destroy the power of egoism and hatred, and develop our capacity for love. It offers to the Father all the energies of mankind and of the universe, all the joys, the hopes, the sorrows, the sufferings, the revolts, the attempts of man to build a better world, more just, more brotherly. And so our Eucharistic celebration is a constant protestation against any structure marked by sin and egoism, and a commitment of our energies to the service of mankind. The Eucharist will not leave us in peace as long as the face of Christ is disfigured in the body and heart of man; it obliges us to hear the voice of the poor, the suffering, and the oppressed, as the very voice of Christ himself (Mt 25:31-46). It gives us life in order that we may become bearers of life and reconciliation, and communicate some of the hope which buoys our own life.

We must evidently, above all and as a necessary condition, be ourselves Eucharistic people, profoundly penetrated by the presence of Christ and his saving mystery. We will not be able to give what we do not possess. On the other hand, on whatever specious pretext, we cannot close ourselves within walls which would prevent us from seeing man's true problems and hearing his urgent call. Our Masses could become practically a call to atheism, if we remained indifferent to the demands of social justice. We must not only be seen united in our churches for Mass and the sacraments but also at the side of our brothers who seek redress and justice. On the other hand, the poor and disinherited must little by little be made to experience the transfiguring presence of the risen Christ in man's heart. In our highly materialized world, the Eucharistic presence of Christ among us as a center of interior peace and contemplation may be at first a sign which is completely incomprehensible but it should sooner or later have the beneficial influence which is the purpose of the sacrament.

The Christian community built up by the Eucharist cannot exist for itself and closed up from the world community in which it exists. Before the world it must be an expression of a love which manifests Christ's presence among men. We are not living fully the Eucharist if we do not freely accept the risks of a Eucharistic life, especially the disturbing voice of God which is the voice of the poor, demanding freedom and the right to live one's human vocation. The Eucharist is a dangerous, indigestible food for anyone who would disregard the true aspiration of man, but also a wonderful if difficult adventure obliging us to befriend the rejected and the outcast, those who need to renew faith in themselves and in mankind, before they can have faith in God and their savior, Jesus Christ.

To celebrate the Eucharist is also to learn to live Christ's resurrection, the contagious hope of a better world to come. It is to witness to this by our faith and our action; to believe in a life that can surmount all obstacles; to love life, to foster its manifestations and nurture its growth. To celebrate the Eucharist is to proclaim the value of Christian joy and hope, their irresistible power against misunderstanding and even failure. Sad songs should give way for the proclamation of the gospel of a loving God (1 Jn 4:8) and of our risen savior. The Paschal mystery must be seen and lived in its totality; the death of Christ and the sin of man are complemented by Christ's glorious resurrection which is radically also that of man.

By the Eucharist we live as resurrected people loosening little by little the grip of our fears, conquering the power of death, fostering the growth of youth and of life. A Eucharistic life is a life of hope and a challenge to the nuisance of pessimism and the corrosion of doubt, and notwithstanding failures, struggles and even a hatred or at least opposition accumulated in the heart of men. This is impossible unless we translate into our daily life the privileged experience of our Eucharistic celebration.

To proclaim Jesus Christ with faith and in love and joy is proper to every sacrament but especially to the Eucharist which is a feast, a celebration of love. Our Eucharists will truly proclaim this joy only if we bear in our heart the presence of the risen Christ. And all the joys, the hopes, and the powers of life and of man's creativity must be part of the Eucharist and find in it an authentic expression.

To put it briefly, Christ especially in the Eucharist is the sacrament of our encounter with God, and the Church is the sacrament of Christ, a sacred means instituted by Christ to signal out his own. But both of these signs need to be complemented by us men as we become the sacrament both of the Church and of Christ. It is by us that Christ will emerge in human life, not in the abstract but in the concrete of our human existence as we become the hope of the poor and engage relentlessly in the struggle for justice against the forces of oppression, alienation and death. This negative approach to Christian love is the first step which leads ultimately to the heights where dwells our God, who is love (1 Jn 4:8). We must humanize people before they can be evangelized and sacramentalized, in relation especially with the center of all the sacraments, the celebration of the Holy Eucharist. This is living the total Eucharistic mystery.

An Interesting Thought

The publication you have just finished reading is part of the apostolic efforts of the Society of St. Paul of the American Province. A small, unique group of priests and brothers, the members of the Society of St. Paul propose to bring the message of Christ to men through the communications media while living the religious life.

If you know of a young man who might be interested in learning more about our life and mission, ask him to contact the Vocation Office in care of ALBA HOUSE, at 2187 Victory Blvd., Staten Island, New York 10314. Full information will be sent without cost or obligation. You may be instrumental in helping a young man to find his vocation in life. *An interesting thought.*

Mon. 6-27-78